...m. we found our Chohuinnish
family. the indians brough
...e oposite side of the river
...le here. this horse had be...
...n our other horses above
...ian information been in
... weeks. while at dinner an
...ently threw a poor half starve...
...it by way of derision far
...very heartily at his own
...had at his insolence that I
... it with great violence
...the breast and face, siezed
...im by signs if he repeated

LEWIS & CLARK

LEWIS & CLARK

An American Journey

Daniel B. Thorp

MetroBooks

MetroBooks

An Imprint of the Michael Friedman Publishing Group, Inc.

Library of Congress Cataloging-in-Publication Data

Thorp, Daniel B.
    Lewis and Clark : an American journey / by Daniel B. Thorp.
      p.   cm.
    Includes bibliographical references and index.
    ISBN 1-56799-584-5
    1. Lewis and Clark Expedition (1804-1806) 2. West (U.S.)—
Discovery and exploration. 3. Lewis and Clark Expedition
(1804-1806)—Pictorial works. 4. West (U.S.)—Discovery and
exploration—Pictorial works. I. Title.
F592.7.T49   1998
917.804′2—dc21

98-12948

Editor: Celeste Sollod
Art Director: Kevin Ullrich
Photography Editor: Sarah Storey
Production Manager: Susan Kowal

Color separations by Bright Arts Graphics (S) Pte Ltd
Printed in Singapore by Tien Wah Press (Pte) Ltd

3 5 7 9 10 8 6 4

For bulk purchases and special sales, please contact:
Michael Friedman Publishing Group, Inc.
Attention: Sales Department
230 Fifth Avenue
New York, NY 10001
212/685-6610 FAX 212/685-1307

Visit our website:
www.metrobooks.com

*The chapter opener illustrations throughout the book are three of the dozens of small sketches Lewis and Clark made in their
journals: a vine maple, a new species discovered at Fort Clatsop; a starry flounder, caught at the mouth of the Columbia
River; and an "ibex," or bighorn sheep, from the Missouri River valley in Montana.*

Dedication

For my mother, Nancy Thorp

Acknowledgments

I want to thank my wife, Elizabeth, for her valuable help in this project. She may think that her greatest contribution came through her willingness to read the book as I wrote it and to make sure that I continued telling a story. But I also want to thank her for letting me go camping with Lewis and Clark when I was supposed to be helping us move.

CONTENTS

Lewis & Clark Expedition
1804–1806

PACIFIC OCEAN

WASHINGTON

Columbia River

Fort Clatsop
salt works

Columbia River

OREGON

Snake River

Lewis' fight with the Blackfeet

Marias River

Travelers' Rest:
Lewis and Clark
parted here on
the return trip

Great Falls

MONTANA

Lolo Pass

Salmon River

Three Forks

Pompy's
Tower

Tongue River

IDAHO

WYOM

CALIFORNIA

NEVADA

UTAH

LEGEND

Miles

0 25 50   100   200

Journey West ────────

Return Journey ════════

LAKE SUPERIOR

• Corps' reunion

• Fort Mandan

Yellowstone River

MINNESOTA

NORTH
DAKOTA

WISCONSIN

SOUTH
DAKOTA

Big Cheyenne River

...er River

• Sgt. Floyd's
grave

IOWA

NEBRASKA

Missouri River

Mississippi River

Platte River

G

LORADO

St. Louis

KANSAS

MISSOURI

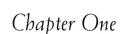

Chapter One

The President Looks West

I T OFTEN SEEMS THAT LEWIS AND CLARK NEED NO INTRO-
duction. For nearly two centuries they have occupied a
special place in the history and mythology of the United
States. Like Washington at Valley Forge, Lincoln at
Gettysburg, and Martin Luther King on the steps of the
Lincoln Memorial, their names are fixed in our national mem-
ory and instantly bring to mind heroic images first encountered in elementary school. Such images often arrive in isola-
tion, though—as if Meriwether Lewis simply woke up one
morning and decided to head west after breakfast. In fact, like
most important events, the Lewis and Clark expedition was
part of a great human tapestry in which any significant event
is linked to others before and after it. And like many other
landmarks in the early history of the United States, the Lewis

and Clark Expedition sprang, in part, from the mind of President Thomas Jefferson.

This was the man Americans elected to be their president in the fall of 1800. The election that year was one of the most bitter in American history. Both sides argued that the fate of the nation hung in the balance, and neither the supporters of Jefferson nor those of his opponent, President John Adams, considered any lie too outrageous to tell. If Jefferson were elected, claimed the Adams camp, the atheism and guillotines of the French Revolution would spread to the United States of America. If Adams were elected, responded the Jeffersonians, he secretly planned to establish an American monarchy, with his son John Quincy as crown prince, and a hereditary nobility. In the end, Jefferson won. The Revolution of 1800, Jeffersonians believed, saved the republic. No sooner had Jefferson taken office, though, than another threat appeared. This one involved the West and it led directly to the Lewis and Clark Expedition.

When Thomas Jefferson looked west he saw the future of America. He was certainly not the first to believe that a nation's wealth and glory followed the sun; Christopher Columbus, Ferdinand Magellan, and a host of others had looked west before him. But to the new American president the stakes were greater than they had ever been before. For him the West was critical to the success of the republic he had helped to found, and it was threatened now by British power as it had not been since the darkest days of the American Revolution. Sending Americans to the Pacific, therefore, was critical to reducing that threat.

Thomas Jefferson

Jefferson himself was a child of what was then the American West. He had been born on the frontier of Virginia. His father, Peter Jefferson, was one of the earliest European settlers in what later became Albemarle County, and was also a surveyor and coauthor of the finest map

ever produced in colonial Virginia. Though the Jeffersons were part of the local elite, young Thomas grew up in a world that still included Indians, wild animals, and adventurous men exploring the West. That frontier mentality stayed with him. Though he went east to Williamsburg for his education and became one of America's great Enlightenment thinkers, he never lost his sense of wonder at the geography, the animals, and the native peoples of the wide open West.

Jefferson did not, however, see the West as a natural wonder to be preserved in its original state. He wanted to develop it in ways that would promote the political and social ideals he had expressed so eloquently in the Declaration of Independence. To ensure that white American men continued to enjoy "life, liberty, and the pursuit of happiness," Jefferson wanted a republic of yeoman farmers and small craftsmen. In his view, only men who worked for themselves and worked with their hands could be trusted to preserve an honest, democratic government. Tenant farmers and factory workers, he thought, would vote the way their landlords or their bosses told them to and would elect a government that served the interests of a moneyed elite—would-be aristocrats determined to crush the democratic ideals of the American Revolution. To ensure that never happened, Jefferson needed land and access to markets. Only if the nation had immense reserves of land would future generations of white Americans be able to establish family farms. And only if those family farms had access to world markets, to the crowded cities of Europe and Asia, would their owners be able to sell their crops, earn a living, and enjoy genuine independence.

Throughout the 1780s and 1790s Jefferson had struggled to realize his dream for America. He was a driving force behind the land ordinances of 1785 and 1787, through which Congress tried to promote his yeoman republic. Under these laws, the American West—from the Appalachian Mountains to the Mississippi River—would be divided into

ALEXANDER MACKENZIE

Born on the Isle of Lewis in Scotland's Outer Hebrides Islands, Alexander Mackenzie came to America at the age of ten, in 1774, when his father decided that New York held greater economic promise than the Hebrides did. Unfortunately, the family arrived in New York just as the colony exploded in revolution, and the elder Mackenzie backed the losing side—joining the king's Royal Regiment of New York in 1776 and serving until his death four years later. Meanwhile, Alexander had been sent to the safer and friendlier environment of Montreal, and there, in 1779, he entered the Canadian fur trade.

After five years in a Montreal office, Mackenzie convinced his employers to send him west in 1784. He quickly proved himself an able trader and in 1785 was offered both a share in the company and a post farther west. By 1787 Mackenzie was part of the newly enlarged North West Company and was sent to the Athabasca River, in central Alberta, as second in command to Peter Pond, then the company's premier western explorer. One year later Mackenzie succeeded Pond as commander on the Athabasca and over the next five years embarked on a stunning series of exploratory voyages on behalf of the North West Company. Following Pond's mistaken car-

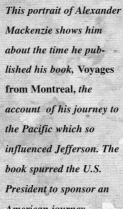

This portrait of Alexander Mackenzie shows him about the time he published his book, **Voyages from Montreal,** *the account of his journey to the Pacific which so influenced Jefferson. The book spurred the U.S. President to sponsor an American journey.*

tography, he first descended what was later named the Mackenzie River to the Arctic Ocean, and then, in 1792–1793, he successfully reached the Pacific and returned to the Athabasca—covering some twenty-three hundred miles (3,700km) without losing a man or firing a shot in anger.

Soon after his return from the Pacific, Mackenzie went back to Montreal. He spent the next five years trying unsuccessfully to convince company and British officials to establish an integrated trading network that would import British goods through Hudson's Bay, trade them for furs among the natives of the Canadian interior, and export the furs to China via the Pacific coast. Promoting this idea was one of the reasons Mackenzie left for England in 1799 to publish his *Voyages from Montreal...to the Frozen and Pacific Oceans*, which Jefferson read so eagerly when he received it in 1802.

Mackensie, by then, had been knighted for his service. In the decade that followed, Sir Alexander occasionally returned to Canada, where he briefly entered politics, and continued his effort to reorganize the fur trade. In 1812 he married a teenage Scottish heiress and retired to her family's estate. He died in Scotland in 1820—one year before Britain established an integrated fur trade in Canada.

millions of family farms organized into townships and states that were guaranteed democratic institutions. It would, Jefferson hoped, preserve his vision of America for generations to come.

He was also a tireless champion of small government and low taxes. As a member of Washington's cabinet and as John Adams' vice president, he waged but often lost a series of battles with Alexander Hamilton to protect American farmers from a legion of tax collectors poised like hungry crows to devour farmers' crops.

Prior to 1800 Thomas Jefferson twice supported efforts by adventurous men to explore the American West. In 1786, when he was U.S. ambassador to France, Jefferson met and encouraged John Ledyard, an English adventurer who planned to travel overland from Paris through Russia and Siberia to North America and cross the continent from west to east. Catherine the Great put an end to this when her government arrested Ledyard in Siberia and deported him. Seven years later, in 1793,

Jefferson tried again. This time he helped coordinate efforts by the American Philosophical Society to send André Michaux, a French botanist, overland from Philadelphia to the Pacific coast—efforts that ended when Jefferson learned Michaux was actually a French spy and demanded that Paris recall him.

Alexander Mackenzie

What prompted Jefferson to dispatch this first American expedition to cross the continent by land was the publication in 1801 of a small book detailing the first British expedition to reach the Pacific from Canada. Citizens of the United States often assume that Lewis and Clark were the first white men to cross North America by land. Canadians know they were not. In the late eighteenth century two rival companies, the Hudson's Bay Company and the North West Company, were competing furiously to dominate the fur trade in what are now western Canada and the United States. Each

In 1802, when Thomas Jefferson first asked Meriwether Lewis to cross North America, the United States ended at the Mississippi. Beyond that river, various countries claimed the land of the North American continent for themselves, making the proposed journey politically as well as physically perilous.

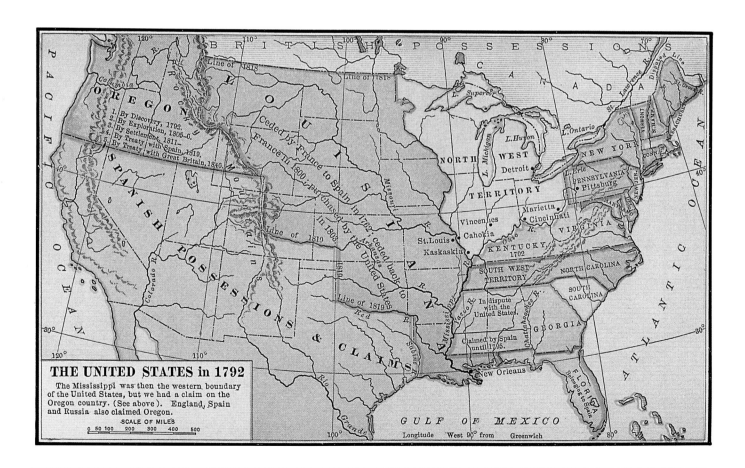

THE UNITED STATES in 1792

The Mississippi was then the western boundary of the United States, but we had a claim on the Oregon country. (See above). England, Spain and Russia also claimed Oregon.

SCALE OF MILES

0 50 100 200 300 400 500

firm sought new sources of fur deeper and deeper in the North American wilderness and established trading posts to collect the furs from Native American hunters. At one of those posts in what is now Alberta, Alexander Mackenzie, a member of the North West Company, began to wonder just how much farther it was to the Pacific coast—which James Cook, George Vancouver, and other English seamen had been exploring since the 1770s. He talked to older company men and to Indians about western geography, and in 1789 he set out to find a route to the Pacific.

His first effort failed when the river he was following, now named the Mackenzie, turned north and took him to the shores of the Arctic Ocean. Undaunted, Mackenzie tried again in 1792. This time his luck was better. Following the Peace River and its tributaries, he reached and easily crossed the Continental Divide. Once on the western slope of the Rockies he struck the upper reaches of the Fraser River and hoped it would lead him to the coast. He soon discovered, however, that the Fraser's canyon was impassable; following directions provided by a group of Indians he met along the way, he set out overland and reached the Dean Channel, on the coast of British Columbia, in July 1793. There he left his name, the date, and a brief description of his historic accomplishment: "from Canada, by land." It was another eight years before he published a full account of his journey, and a year after that Thomas Jefferson received a copy in the United States.

Reading Mackenzie's story must have thrilled and frightened Jefferson simultaneously. The westerner and naturalist in him would have marveled at Mackenzie's accomplishment and at the natural wonders he had seen. Virginians had been searching for a route to "the Western Waters" since the founding of Jamestown nearly two centuries before, and Alexander Mackenzie had finally found one. But as president of the United States, Jefferson must have shuddered at the notion of British trappers, soldiers, and settlers following in Mackenzie's footsteps and gaining control of the northern Pacific coast. For the past decade ships from many nations, including the United States, had visited the coast of British Columbia and obtained in trade sea otter pelts worth a small fortune in China. At the moment, none of these outside powers actually controlled the Pacific Northwest, but Mackenzie gave Britain a powerful claim to the region and the inside track in the race to exercise effective control there.

The American Response

Jefferson had to act. The United States would have to meet Mackenzie's challenge and go the British one better. Mackenzie had crossed the Rockies but had failed to discover any river that would take him to the coast. An American captain, Robert Gray, had already found the mouth of the Columbia River in 1792. It was a massive river that must surely reach inland to the Rockies. If other Americans could ascend the Missouri River and reach the Columbia from the east, they might find what Mackenzie had missed: an effective water route from the American heartland to the Pacific coast and the markets of Asia. The fact that the Missouri flowed through Spanish territory did not bother Jefferson in the least. He had long believed that the Spanish empire was a hollow shell and hoped that Americans would eventually cross the Mississippi and expand into the Missouri Valley, conquering the Spanish borderlands without firing a shot. When that happened a practical link to the Pacific would enable American settlers to trade with Asia, extending Jefferson's agrarian society into the West and preserving the yeoman republic he envisioned.

Late in 1802 Jefferson approached Carlos Martínez de Yrujo, the Spanish minister in Washington D.C., about "a small caravan" of Americans crossing the region between the mouth of the Missouri and the Pacific coast in search of "a continual communication, or little interrupted, by water as far as the South Sea."

The President Looks West

Would the Spanish court "take it badly," wondered Jefferson? According to Martínez, Jefferson saw no reason for the Spanish to have "the least fear" from such an expedition because its only purpose would be to advance scientific and geographic knowledge. Jefferson might announce that the caravan was seeking to advance "the progress of commerce," but

that, he assured Martínez, would simply be a cover to justify congressional funding for the project. Surely Spain would not object to such a noble undertaking. Spain did object, though. Martínez told the president "that an expedition of this nature could not fail to give umbrage to our Government." Besides, he told Jefferson, numerous explorers, including "the celebrated

perpetuate the fame of his administration...by discovering or attempting at least to discover the way by which the Americans may some day extend their population and their influence up to the coasts of the South Sea."

A Request to Congress

Martínez knew his man. Whatever the Spanish court might think or do, Jefferson had already made up his mind. It was already well known that Spain was trading Louisiana to France; Jefferson was about to nominate American emissaries to discuss with France the sale of New Orleans and some of the territory around it to the United States; other Americans were calling for war to seize New Orleans from the French; and no one knew how Great Britain, the traditional enemy of France and recent enemy of the United States, would react to any of this. However events played out, Jefferson wanted an American party to reach the Pacific as soon as possible. So in January 1803, just a month after discussing his idea with the Spanish ambassador, Jefferson sent Congress a confidential message requesting funds for the exploring project.

His message was carefully written to describe the expedition in terms that would make it appropriate to the limited government of Jefferson's day. Americans then still had vivid memories of Parliament and George III trying to smother local government in America, and as a result many people in and out of Congress were determined to keep the central government on a very short leash. The Constitution did, however, give Congress clear authority over Indian affairs and Indian trade, and Jefferson combined the two in justifying his request for funds.

It was only a matter of time, the president wrote, before Indians east of the Mississippi became settled farmers, and it was Washington's duty to encourage this transition by establishing government trading posts to accept their surplus crops and "place within

Jefferson's beloved home, Monticello, stood on a mountain in Virginia's Albemarle County. The site offered Jefferson a sweeping view to the west, and, after the expedition, he filled the house with a number of specimens brought back by Lewis and Clark.

Makensi," had already shown conclusively that no such route existed between the Missouri and the Pacific.

Martínez hoped that he had convinced Jefferson to drop the scheme, but still he worried: "The President has been all his life a man of letters, very speculative and a lover of glory, and it would be possible he might attempt to

their reach those things which will contribute more to their domestic comfort." Government trading posts would drive out private traders, though, because the nonprofit government stores could operate more cheaply, and Jefferson suggested that Congress provide another outlet for "the enterprize of these citizens." That other outlet was the Missouri River and the natives living along it. Private American traders could shift their business west and trade with western tribes via the Missouri much more effectively than their British rivals could from Canada. The harsh Canadian climate, Jefferson claimed, "could bear no competition with that of the Missouri, traversing a moderate climate, offering according to the best accounts a continued navigation from it's source, and, possibly with a single portage, from the Western ocean."

There was the prize Jefferson sought—a practical route to the Pacific—and Congress could make it happen. "An intelligent officer with ten or twelve chosen men," he predicted, "might explore the whole line, even to the Western ocean, have conferences with the natives on the subject of commercial intercourse, get admission among them for our traders...and return with the information acquired in the course of two summers." And it could all be possible if Congress would simply provide $2,500 for "their arms & accoutrements, some instruments of observation, & light & cheap presents for the Indians" ($2,500 was actually about one-sixteenth of Lewis and Clark's final reckoning of their trip's total cost to the government).

Members considered the president's request for a month and quietly approved it in late February. Jefferson had the authorization he wanted for an American expedition to the Pacific, and, unbeknownst to Congress, he already had a man to lead it.

January 18, 1803. While other civilized nations have encountered great expense to enlarge the boundaries of knowledge, by undertaking voyages of discovery, & for other literary purposes, in various parts and directions, our nation seems to owe to the same object, as well as to its own interest, to explore this, the only line of easy communication across the continent, and so directly traversing our own part of it.

Thomas Jefferson

Views like this, from Virginia's Hawksbill Mountain, led men such as Jefferson to imagine that the Rockies would be like the Appalachians— relatively low and easy to cross. They were not.

Chapter Two

Plans and Preparations

JEFFERSON HAD PROBABLY SETTLED ON HIS PRIVATE secretary, Meriwether Lewis, to command the expedition before he ever approached Congress. He had known Lewis almost since the latter's birth in 1774. William Lewis, Meriwether's father, had been a neighbor of Jefferson's in Albemarle County, and Jefferson, whose own sons had died in infancy, may have seen young Lewis as a surrogate son. Lewis spent his childhood on frontier plantations in Virginia and Georgia, where he developed a keen love of the wilderness and sharp skills for surviving in it. He also enjoyed several years of schooling with tutors from whom he learned reading, writing, and arithmetic. When he came of age in 1792, he established himself as a planter on land he had inherited in Virginia, but two years later he left it for the life of a soldier.

Lewis' Qualifications

In 1794 farmers in Pennsylvania took up arms against an excise tax on the whiskey they made. President Washington sent the army to suppress the rebels and called on state militias to augment the regular army. Among the volunteers from Virginia was Meriwether Lewis. The campaign itself was something of a farce. Government forces were ill-trained and badly equipped, and both weather and terrain often worked against them. Even the rebels refused to cooperate, vanishing without a fight before the army could cover itself with military glory. Lewis, however, had a wonderful time—writing to his mother that he was enjoying the manly company and the "oceans of Whiskey." Not surprisingly, when the rebellion ended he volunteered to stay on as part of a militia force keeping order in western Pennsylvania. From there he moved to the regular army as an ensign in 1795, and was soon posted to the Ohio Country, where most of the army spent its time keeping an eye on the Native American population.

For the next five years Lewis served in a series of frontier posts. It was generally a quiet period in the army. There was no war to speak of, in spite of worsening relations with France and a quasi-war with the French navy, so the only fighting Lewis saw was among the soldiers themselves—including himself. In 1795 he was involved in a drunken argument with a fellow officer that escalated to a dueling challenge and a court-martial in which Lewis was eventually acquitted. During his years in the army the young Virginian served in a variety of capacities ranging from courier to paymaster, rose in rank to captain, and gained an intimate knowledge of what was then the Far West of the United States. And it was there, in early 1801, that he received a letter from President-elect Jefferson inviting him to Washington, D.C., as the new chief executive's private secretary.

Jefferson chose Lewis to be his secretary because he felt the young man's "knolege of the Western country, of the army and of all it's interests & relations" suited him to the task. Two years later, in 1803, those same attributes were part of what made him Jefferson's choice to recruit and lead an expedition up the Missouri. At age twenty-eight, Meriwether Lewis came as close as any man Jefferson knew to combining the mental and physical skills it would take to meet the challenge before him. In a letter to the mathematician Robert Patterson, Jefferson compared Lewis to his ideal candidate:

> If we could have got a person perfectly skilled in botany, natural history, mineralogy, [and] astronomy, with at the same time the necessary firmness of body & mind, habits of living in the woods & familiarity with the Indian character, it would have been better. But I know of no such character who would undertake an enterprise so perilous. To all the latter qualities Capt. Lewis joins a great stock of accurate observation on the subjects of the three kingdoms [animal, vegetable, and mineral] found in our country but not according to their scientific nomenclatures. But he will be able to seize for examination & description such things only as he shall meet with new. He has [also] been for some time qualifying himself for taking observations of longitude & latitude to fix the geographical points of the line he will pass over.

It is true that at least one member of Jefferson's cabinet felt that Lewis might be too impulsive. The attorney general, Levi Lincoln, thought Lewis "will be more likely, in case of difficulty, to push too far than to rec[e]de too soon," but the president had every confidence in Captain Lewis.

Jefferson's Instructions

Through the spring and summer of 1803, Jefferson and Lewis worked feverishly to get

the expedition under way. Jefferson wrote letters of introduction to several American scientists from whom he hoped Lewis could obtain further instruction and secured passports for Lewis from the French and British governments permitting the American and his troops to cross their territory.

The president's most significant contribution to the preparations was his instructions to Lewis because they laid out clearly what the nation expected of him. In no uncertain terms he reminded Lewis that the chief purpose of this mission was to find "the most direct & practicable water communication across this continent for the purposes of commerce" and to ensure that Washington received accurate information about it. Toward that end, it was critical that he take careful note of the latitude and longitude of all "remarkable points" between the mouth of the Missouri and the coast of the Pacific, make several copies of his observations, and "put [them] into the care of the most trust-worthy of your attendants, to guard...against the accidental losses to which they will be exposed." On reaching the Pacific, Lewis was to learn if ships from any nation frequented that coast and, if it were practical, to send two of the party back by sea with a copy of his notes. The rest of the men, and Lewis himself, were then to return by land or sea "as you shall be able." Jefferson also warned Lewis not to take unnecessary risks and assured him that "we value too much the lives of our citizens to offer them to probable destruction." But the instructions suggest that Jefferson valued what Lewis might learn at least as much as he valued the man himself: "In the loss of yourselves, we should lose also the information you will have acquired. By returning safely with that [even if he failed to reach the coast], you may enable us to renew the essay with better calculated means."

The president's instructions also show that Lewis had another job as well. He was to be Jefferson's roving ambassador to the western Indians and, like any ambassador, was to conduct research as well as diplomacy. He was directed to collect as much information as he could about the Indian nations through which he passed, inquiring about their numbers and territory, of course, but also about their languages, customs, clothing, housing, religion, and what items they might wish to trade or buy from the United States. And wherever he went, Lewis was to meet with native leaders, "make them acquainted with...our wish to be neighborly, friendly & useful to them," and help to arrange reciprocal visits by Indian leaders to Washington. These obligations, however, extended only "as far as a diligent pursuit of your journey shall admit." Nothing was to interfere with Lewis' principal goal: finding a practical route to the Pacific.

Supplies

Lewis, in the meantime, spent the spring of 1803 trying to anticipate every material need that might arise on the expedition. What did one take for a two-year journey through a region no white man had ever crossed? Echoing Jefferson's priorities, Lewis thought first of surveying equipment: a quadrant, a compass, a theodolite (a telescopic device used by surveyors to measure angles), and assorted paraphernalia. Next came guns and ammunition—certainly for hunting, but for defense if necessary. He planned to carry little in the way of food or clothing; the party would take some liquor (standard military rations at the time) and 150 pounds (68kg) of "portable soup"—a dried or condensed soup—as emergency rations, and each man would need an overcoat, a raincoat, a pair of overalls, several shirts, and two pairs of socks. Obviously, Lewis planned from the start for his men to feed and clothe themselves by hunting along the way. They could not expect to find tools on their journey, though, so Lewis included a long list of pots, axes, drills, files, and other equipment for the trek. He also planned to transport hundreds of pounds of "Indian Presents": beads of various colors, needles, knives, fishhooks, cloth, and dozens of other items intended to smooth the diplomatic process and spark native interest in trade with the Americans. Finally, the expedition would need transportation—a keelboat and a canoe—and a variety of medicines.

To fill these needs Lewis spent most of the spring traveling. His first stop was the federal arsenal at Harper's Ferry, Virginia. There he could find guns, of course, but his major objec-tive in Harper's Ferry was to investigate an iron canoe frame. Though no one but Indians knew exactly what Lewis would encounter as he ascended the Missouri, it was obvious to any frontiersman that at some point or points the expedition would have to leave the larger boats in which it began the journey and rely on smaller boats or travel by land. This, plus the volume of the party's equipment, convinced

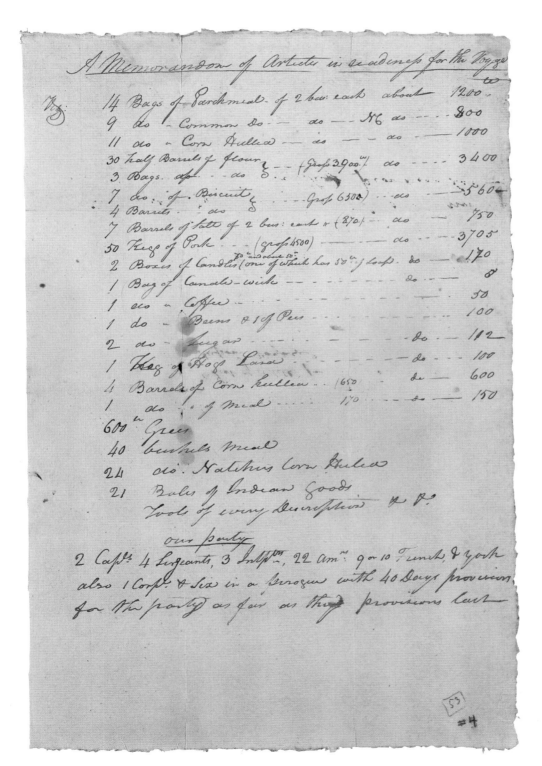

Shortly before leaving Camp Dubois, William Clark compiled this list of some of the items carried by the expedition. At the bottom of the page he also provided a description of the men in the party that explains why historians still cannot agree on its exact composition: Clark mentioned "4 Sergeants," instead of three, and "9 or 10 French."

Plans and Preparations

Under Lewis' supervision, artisans at Harper's Ferry built and tested two sections of an iron canoe frame that could be carried until needed and then assembled for use with a hide or bark exterior. It took nearly a month to conduct the test, and the finished sections weighed more than Lewis had estimated they would, but still he was pleased with the results and ordered the canoe's completion.

Lewis he would need something larger than the sort of canoes they could make on the spot and easier to transport around unnavigable stretches. He wanted the smiths at Harper's Ferry to construct and test a set of iron ribs for a forty-foot (12m)-long canoe. If the experiment worked, the preconstructed frame could be carried until it was needed and then be assembled, covered with hides or bark, and used. Afterward it could be disassembled, carried, and reassembled as often as necessary.

The canoe took nearly a month to complete, much longer than Lewis had planned, and the workers required close personal attention "to understand the design perfectly," but the results were worth the effort. According to Lewis, the new boat would be far superior to a traditional canoe of the same size. "It is much stronger," he wrote, "will carry its burthen with equal ease, and greater security; and when the bark and wood are discarded, will be much lighter, and can be transported with more safety and ease." Flush with success, he instructed the workers to complete the frame while he went on to Philadelphia—then the nation's largest city and home to many of the scientists with whom Jefferson wanted him to meet before his departure.

In Philadelphia Lewis combined a series of educational interviews with a shopping trip of epic proportions. His longest visits seem to have been with Andrew Ellicott, an astronomer, and Robert Patterson, a professor of mathematics at the University of Pennsylvania. Patterson had already developed for Lewis' use an astronomical formula for computing longitude through observations of the moon, and now the two experts discussed with Lewis the easiest way for a relative novice such as he to secure the geographical information the president required: abandon the theodolite, which was "difficult of transportation, and...liable to get out of order," in favor of a sextant. Lewis also met with Benjamin Rush, one of the nation's most eminent physicians as well as a celebrated natural historian, to discuss what sorts of information Lewis should seek from

and about the Indians he met and medical guidelines to preserve the health of his men ("flannel should be worn constantly next to the skin"). Most of Lewis' time in Philadelphia must have been spent shopping, though. He visited dozens of businesses in the city—druggists, coppersmiths, shoe- and saddlemakers, and a number of general merchants. In all, he spent more than $2,000 before returning to Washington in June.

William Clark

For Lewis there remained one crucial decision to make before heading west. He had already written to army commanders in the Ohio Valley and asked them to identify potential candidates for the expedition which, for security reasons, he told them was going up the Mississippi. Now Jefferson wanted him to name a successor in order to prevent "anarchy, dispersion, & the consequent danger to your party" in case of Lewis' death. That necessity prompted Lewis to send one of the most remarkable letters in American history. On June 19, 1803, he wrote to a former army buddy, in strictest confidence, describing in great detail the actual project he was about to undertake and how he proposed to do it. Then came the truly remarkable part:

> *Thus my friend you have so far as leisure will at this time permit me to give it you, a summary view of the plan, the means and the object of this expedition. If therefore there is anything under those circumstances, in this enterprise, which would induce you to participate with me in it's fatiegues, it's dangers and it's honors, believe me there is no man on earth with whom I should feel equal pleasure in sharing them than with yourself.*

The former army buddy was, of course, William Clark, and Lewis asked him to join the expedition as a co-commander. Clark would

Plans and Preparations
29

also be a captain, and, wrote Lewis, "your situation if joined with me in this mission will in all respects be precisely such as my own."

The man who inspired such trust was four years older than Lewis and even more experienced in life on the frontier. Though born in Virginia in 1770, Clark had moved to Kentucky with his parents in 1784. There he was reunited with his older brother, George Rogers Clark, who had become both a general and a legend through his exploits fighting the British and their Indian allies in the Ohio Valley during the American Revolution. By the early 1790s William was marching in his brother's footsteps, participating in a number of militia campaigns against Native Americans and earning a reputation as "a youth of solid and promising parts and as brave as Caesar." In 1792 he sought a place in the regular army and was commissioned a lieutenant of infantry. During the next four years he served with General Anthony Wayne, participating in the latter's 1794 campaign against a loose confederacy of Miami, Shawnee, Delaware, and other Indian tribes, and for part of that time, in 1795 and 1796, Meriwether Lewis was under Clark's direct command.

William left the army in 1796 and returned to his family's plantation outside Louisville, where he began helping his brother, George Rogers, attempt to settle the latter's tangled business affairs. There Lewis' letter found him in July, and he responded to it the next day. "This is an undertaking fraited with many difeculties," wrote Clark, "but my Friend I do assure you that no man lives whith whome I would perfur to undertake Such a Trip &c. as your self."

Delays and Complications

Back in Washington, D.C., with no way of knowing what Clark would decide, Lewis made final preparations for his departure, including a not-very-honest letter to his mother. "The day

after tomorrow I shall set out for the Western Country," he wrote. He assured her that he felt "perfectly prepared" for the adventure and, like any son, lied shamelessly about the risks he would face: "The nature of this expedition is by no means dangerous, my rout will be altogether through tribes of Indians who are perfectly friendly to the United States, [and I] therefore consider the chances of life just as much in my favor on this trip as I should conceive them were I to remain at home for the same length of time." He actually remained in Washington a few extra days, just long enough to be there for Jefferson's formal announcement that the United States had purchased the whole of Louisiana from France, which meant that most of his journey would now be across American rather than foreign territory. Finally, on July 5, 1803, Meriwether Lewis left for the Pacific.

From Washington, D.C., Lewis set out for Pittsburgh—the gateway to the West. There he planned to receive the equipment being shipped from Philadelphia and Harper's Ferry, load it onto a boat being built for him in Pittsburgh, and start down the Ohio by early August. At every stage, though, delays and complications forced the impatient Lewis to wait. Passing through Harper's Ferry, he found that the wagon from Philadelphia had not picked up the weapons and canoe frame waiting at the arsenal, so Lewis himself had to arrange their transportation. Once he got to Pittsburgh, he found that the boat he expected to be ready by July 20 was nowhere close to

OPPOSITE: *William Clark— red-headed, thirty-two years old, and an experienced woodsman—was Lewis' first choice as co-commander of the expedition. It was an excellent choice. Lewis may have been better suited to inspire the men, but he also suffered from periodic bouts of depression. Clark, shown here in an 1807 painting by Charles Willson Peale, had a steadier disposition and provided a stabilizing presence in the expedition.* ABOVE: *In this letter out of the blue, Meriwether Lewis asked William Clark, whom he had known since their army days, to join him on the trip of a lifetime.*

Located at the junction of the Potomac and Shenandoah Rivers, Harper's Ferry, Virginia, was a modest factory town in 1803. It was home to the United States Army arsenal, and its artisans were among the most skilled machinists in the United States. Lewis turned to the arsenal for the latest model of muskets for his men and to its artisans for help realizing his design for a portable boat. This modern photo of Harper's Ferry National Historic Park shows the arsenal as Lewis would have seen it.

completion. There was little Lewis could do. "I visit him every day," he wrote of the boat-builder, "and endeavor by every means in my power to hasten the completion of the work," but still his departure was delayed—first until early August and then until late August.

The delay may have been providential, though. Had his equipment and boat been ready when Lewis arrived, he might have left Pittsburgh without ever hearing from Clark. When Lewis invited his friend to join the expedition, he asked him to send his response to Pittsburgh. When he arrived there in late July, however, no letter awaited him, and he wrote to the president that if he heard nothing from Clark before his departure from Pittsburgh he planned to ask Lt. Moses Hooke to accompany him as second in command. Hooke, wrote Lewis, was an able young man—"endowed with a good constitution, possessing a sensible well informed mind, is industrious, prudent and per-severing"—and were it not for an oft-delayed boatbuilder, Americans might be celebrating the Lewis and Hooke Expedition. Eight days later Clark's letter arrived, and Lt. Hooke slipped into oblivion.

Down the Ohio

On the morning of August 31, Lewis was final-ly able to leave Pittsburgh for Louisville, where Clark was to join him with "a fiew men, such as will best answer our purpose." Some of the crew traveling with Lewis may also have been invited to join the expedition—Lewis wrote that they were "on trial"—but most were simply soldiers assigned to accompany Lewis down the Ohio. The descent was both slow and difficult. The water was so low that from Pittsburgh as far as Wheeling the river was often blocked by sandbars. Some of these the crew could over-come by unloading the boat and lifting it themselves over the sand and rocks, but in other cases Lewis had to hire farmers to drag the boat over with their oxen. "In this way I have passed as many as five of those bars...in a

THE LOUISIANA PURCHASE

While Meriwether Lewis was preparing for his expedition, another of President Jefferson's initiatives bore unexpected fruit in Paris.

In 1800 Napoleon Bonaparte had pressured Spain into giving France the territory known as Louisiana—everything between the Mississippi River and the Rocky Mountains, from Texas and New Mexico to the Canadian border. Napoleon's principal aim was to use Louisiana as a base from which to support an effort to recapture the rebellious French colony of St. Domingue (Haiti). French control of Louisiana worried Jefferson because France, unlike Spain, was strong enough to defend the territory against American expansion and close the Mississippi to American trade. To prevent this, early in 1803, Jefferson sent American envoys to Europe to negotiate the purchase of New Orleans and the region east of that city.

By the time the Americans reached Paris, though, Napoleon had lost interest in St. Domingue. His commander there had recently died, French troops on the island had been devastated by disease, and his war with Britain was breaking out again after a brief truce. France had no use for Louisiana anymore, but it needed American money and goodwill in the fight against Britain. Thus, when the Americans arrived to negotiate the sale of New Orleans, the French offered them all of Louisiana. The Americans quickly accepted. They had no authorization to do so, and the price, $15,000,000, was more than seven times what Congress had appropriated for the purchase of New Orleans, but the Americans knew a bargain when they saw one. The treaty still had to be ratified by the Senate, and Congress still had to raise the money, but by the time Lewis and Clark started up the Missouri River, it flowed through American territory.

In 1803, just before Lewis set off, the nation doubled its size through the Louisiana Purchase, an acquisition of a great tract of land west of Mississippi. This nineteenth-century map of the United States shows the impact on the nation of the Louisiana Purchase. West of Louisiana, parts of the continent were still claimed by Britain, Spain, and Russia.

day," wrote Lewis, "and [had] to unload as many or more times." The going was somewhat better below Wheeling, but it was still slow and was made slower still by crewmen who were sometimes "so drunk that they were unable to help themselves."

Not until mid-October did Lewis reach Louisville, but there, on October 15, Lewis and Clark joined forces and began to assemble their men. Lewis had written to Clark that he was looking for "stout, healthy, unmarried men, accustomed to the woods, and capable of bearing bodily fatigue in a pretty considerable degree." Two may have come downstream with Lewis; seven others were waiting with Clark.

More joined during the next three months as Lewis and Clark continued down the Ohio, stopping at army posts along the way to meet with men suggested by their commanders as suitable candidates for the expedition. The growing party then ascended the Mississippi to St. Louis and established a winter camp, Camp Dubois, on the east bank of the Mississippi near its junction with the Missouri. Most of the men there were strangers to one another and to their captains, and all were learning now, for the first time, what was really expected of them. Come spring they had to be ready to ascend the Missouri and enter an American West unknown to any white American.

Chapter Three

Up the Missouri

COLLECTIVELY, THEY ARE AMONG THE MOST famous men in American history, but as individuals they are virtually unknown. Their names have been subsumed under those of their famous commanders even though these lesser-known men were as vital to the success of the Lewis and Clark Expedition as any. George Shannon, Joseph Whitehouse, Pierre Cruzatte, Silas Goodrich, and most of the other men who accompanied Lewis and Clark are nameless to any but the most diligent readers of American history. Before they vanished into collective glory, though, they were men with individual strengths and weaknesses, and during the winter of 1803–1804 their commanders tried to evaluate those strengths and weaknesses and assemble an effective Corps of Discovery to head into the West.

NEBRASKA

Platte River

KANSAS

Sgt. Floyd's grave

IOWA

Mississippi River

Missouri River

St. Louis

MISSOURI

PAGE 36: *Sandbars and drifting logs were just two of the problems that Lewis and Clark encountered as they ascended the Missouri. At first they were also working against a current so strong that their boats rarely traveled more than one mile per hour.* ABOVE: *After leaving St. Louis, members of the expedition spent five months, from May to October, 1804, rowing, poling, and towing their boats up the Missouri River to Mandan country.*

Assembling the Men

Some forty men spent the winter in Camp Dubois. About a third were civilians—young Americans recruited in Kentucky by Lewis and Clark or men of French or French-Indian (called métis) blood from the population around St. Louis. The rest were soldiers drawn from posts along the Lower Ohio. They were not "gentlemen"; several of the latter had approached Clark about participating, but he discouraged them on the grounds that "they are not accustomed to labor." Those who were invited to try out were working men: carpenters, blacksmiths, boatmen, farmers, and the like. George Shannon, who was just eighteen, was the youngest man present, and John Shields, at thirty-four, was the oldest; most, however, were in their late twenties or early thirties. Only two are known to have been married at the time. (Although Lewis had told Clark to select only single men, they did accept at least two who were married.) The largest number, at least nine, had been born in Virginia, but there were also natives of Pennsylvania, Massachusetts, New Hampshire, and several other American states; at least one

from Germany; and several from Canada. Wherever they had been born, though, all were living in the Ohio/Mississippi Valley before coming to Camp Dubois. There was also one African-American in camp—William Clark's slave, York, who was about thirty years old that winter.

The men spent winter and early spring preparing for their departure. They modified their boat for its journey up the Missouri by adding a collapsible mast and storage lockers, packed and repacked both the supplies brought from Philadelphia and additional stores bought in St. Louis, drilled, and took target practice from time to time. They also got into trouble. They were young, they were bored, and they drank more than they were supposed to. The result was a number of disciplinary problems, especially one week in February when both Lewis and Clark had to be gone from camp. When Clark got back he found that Reubin Field, one of the men, had refused to stand guard, that others had encouraged this "opposition to the faithfull discharge of his duty...and excited disorder and faction among the party," and that at least one man had threatened to shoot another. Less dramatic, but just as disturbing, was the discovery that a number of men had "made hunting or other business a pretext to cover their design of visiting a neighbouring whiskey shop." Three men were court-martialed for disobedience and four were confined to camp for their unauthorized visits to the whiskey shop.

When not busy maintaining order, the commanders made final preparations for the trip. Lewis made several visits to Spanish officials in St. Louis who remained in charge of Louisiana until March and still felt obliged to block his progress and report his presence to their superiors in New Orleans (who, in turn, issued orders "to arrest Captain Merry Weather and his party"). Nevertheless, Spanish authorities were also willing to provide Lewis with the latest information they had about the people and geography of the Missouri River Valley. Clark spent more time in camp, practicing his

astronomical observations and supervising work on the boat. Both commanders made additional purchases in and around St. Louis, especially of food, and together they chose and organized the men who would actually accompany them to the Pacific.

The "Perminent Detachment"

On April 1, 1804, Clark wrote the order: "The commanding officers did yesterday proceed to take the necessary inlistments and select the Detachment destined for the Expedition through the interior of the Continent of North America." Twenty-six men were enlisted as members of the "Perminent Detachment" to join George Drouillard, a métis interpreter; York, Clark's slave; and Lewis and Clark themselves in crossing the continent. Another four soldiers were retained "untill further orders"; somewhere up the Missouri they would be sent back bearing reports. Three of the men—

Nathaniel Pryor, Charles Floyd, and John Ordway—were promoted to sergeant and placed in command of the three squads into which the enlisted men were divided. The exact composition of the squads and of the "Perminent Detachment" would change in the months to come as men were added or dropped, but the basic structure established at Camp Dubois survived. Small as it was, the Lewis and Clark Expedition was a military body with a recognized chain of command.

At the top of the chain, however, there was a complication. Lewis, with the President's consent, had invited Clark to serve as co-commander and had promised him a captain's commission and pay. When the paperwork reached St. Louis, though, he was startled to discover that Clark had been made a lieutenant. Lewis was furious, feeling that he and Clark had both been deceived, and was worried about the effect it would have on Clark and on military order in the expedition. He immediately wrote to Clark, who was at Camp Dubois, in an effort to put a better face on the news. He pointed

An official payment requi-
sition lists the members of
the Corps of Discovery,
with each one's name,
rank, dates of commence-
ment and ending of ser-
vice, length of service, rate,
and amount finally due.

out to his friend that "the grade has no effect upon the compensation, which by G—d, shall be equal to my own," and told him, "I think it will be best to let none of our party or any other persons know any thing about the grade." As far as Lewis was concerned, they would still be co-commanders.

Clark went along with the deception, but it hurt. Seven years later he told Nicholas Biddle, who was preparing a history of the expedition, "I did not think myself very well treated as I did not get the appointment which was promised me." He accepted the commission and his position "from the assurance of Capt. Lewis, that in every respect my situation Command &c. &c. should be equal to his," but he was clearly still upset by the slight and embarrassed by it. "I have never related as

We the Subscribers do acknowledge to have received of [the several Sums set opposite to our] Names, the Same being due us from the War Department pursuant to an Act of Congress bearing date March the 3rd 1807 intitled "an Act making compensation to Messrs Lewis & Clark and their companions" — Signed Duplicates

No.	Names	Rank	Commencement of service and settlement as per Pay Roll	Ending of pay as per pay Role at the expiration of Service	Time Paid for (Months)	(Days)	Rate per Month	Amount of Pay Received (Dollars)	(Cents)	Signers Names	Witness
1	John Ordway	Sergeant	1 of January 1804	15 of October 1806	33	10	8	266	66 2/3		
2	Nathaniel Pryor	ditto	20 of October 1803	15 of October 1806	35	20	5&8	278	50		
3	Charles Floyd	ditto	1 of August 1803	20 of August 1804	12	20	8	86	33 1/3		
4	Patrick Gass	ditto	1 of January 1804	15 of October 1806	33	10	5&8	243	66 2/3		
5	William Bratton	Private	20 of October 1803	15 of October 1806	35	20	5	178	33 1/3		
7	John Colter	do	15 of October 1803	do do	35	-	5	179	33 1/3		
8	Pierre Cruzatte	do	16 of May 1804	do do	28	25	5	144	16 2/3		
9	Joseph Fields	do	1 of August 1803	do do	38	10	5	19?	16 2/3		
10	Reubin Fields	do	1 of August 1803	do do	38	10	5	191	66 2/3		
11	Robert Frazier	do	1 of January 1804	do do	33	10	5	166	66 2/3		
12	Silas Goodrich	do	1 of Jany 1804	do do	33	10	5	166	66 2/3		
13	George Gibson	do	19 of October 1803	do do	35	21	5	178	50		
14	Thomas P + x							166	66 2/3		
15	Hugh Hall	do	1 of Jany 1804	do do	33	7	5	166	66 2/3		
16	Francis Labiche	do	16 of May 1804	do do	28	5	5	144	66 2/3		
17	Hugh McNeal	do	1 of Jany 1804	do do	33		5	166	66 2/3		
18	John Shields	do	19 of Octob 1803	do do	35	7	5	178	50		
19	George Shannon	do	19 of Oct 1803	do do	35	7	5	178	50		
20	John Potts	do	1 of Jany 1804	do do	33	7	5	166	66 2/3		
21	John Baptiste Lepage	do	2 of Nov 1804	do do	22		5	111	50		
22	John B. Thompson	do	1 of Jany 1804	do do	33		5	166	66 2/3		
23	William Werner	do	1 of Jany 1804	do do	33	7	5	166	66 2/3		
24	Richard Windsor	do	1 of Jany 1804	do do	33	7	5	166	66 2/3		
25	Peter Wiser	do	1 of Jany 1804	do do	33	10	5	166	66 2/3		
26	Alexander Willard	do	1 of Jany 1804	do do	33	10	5	166	66 2/3		
27	Joseph Whitehouse	do	1 of Jany 1804	do do	33	10	5	166	66 2/3		
28	Richard Warfington	Corporal	14 of May 1804	1 of June 1805	12	17	7	99	96 2/3		
29	John Newman	Private	14 of May 1804	1 of June 1805	12	17	5	62	83 1/3		
30	George Druellier	Interpreter	1 of January 1804	15 of October 1806	33	10	25	833	33 1/3		
31	Toussaint Charbono	ditto	7 of April 1805	17 of August 1806	16	11	25	409	16 2/3		

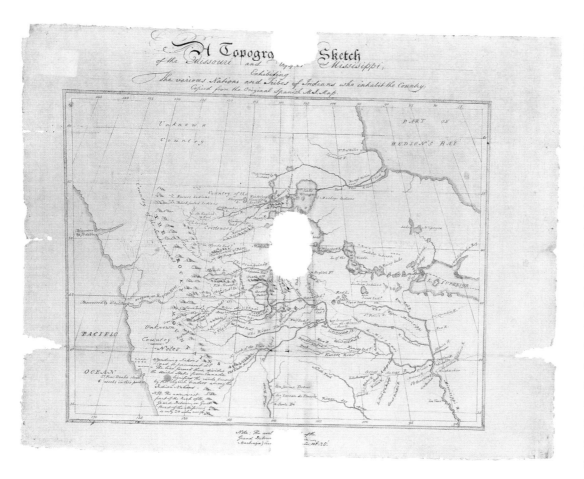

A Topographical Sketch of the Missouri and upper Mississippi, Exhibiting the various Nations and Tribes of Indians who inhabit the Country. Copied from the Original Spanish M.S. Map.

As Lewis and Clark ascended the Missouri, they had with them a map prepared in Washington that offered the latest geographic information on the route they were to follow. The map shows the Missouri for a few hundred miles west of St. Louis and the area immediately around the Mandan villages. What lay between those points, however, was anyone's guess. The map was folded when being carried; the hole in the middle and on the edges demonstrates the wear and tear to which it was subjected.

much on this subject to any person before," he told Biddle. "Be so good as to place me on equal footing with Cap. Lewis in every point of view without exposeing any thing which might have taken place or even mentioning the Commission at all." Whatever he felt or thought in 1804 Clark kept to himself, and as far as their men were concerned Captains Lewis and Clark were co-commanders of the Corps of Discovery.

Setting Off!

In fact, it was actually William Clark who led the small flotilla out of Camp Dubois and started up the Missouri on May 14, 1804 (Lewis would join them at St. Charles, traveling overland from St. Louis six days later). Most of the men were aboard the keelboat that had come down from Pittsburgh. The boat was fifty-five feet (17m) long and eight feet (2.5m) wide. The bow was decked and there was a small cabin at the stern, but the center of the boat

was open—with storage lockers running down each side and benches spanning the gap between them. It was possible to erect an awning over the midships, but otherwise the benches were totally exposed. With the boat were two pirouges, large dugout canoes used in the western fur trade. One was manned by soldiers and the other by French boatmen engaged at St. Louis to help the Corps ascend the Lower Missouri. Every man was armed with a rifle or musket, and there were three swivel guns that could be mounted on the boats. Packed in the boats were the camping equipment and Indian presents bought in Philadelphia, plus additional supplies picked up in St. Louis, especially food. The Corps now carried five tons (4.5t) of parched corn, meal, flour, and pork, more than one hundred gallons (45.5kg) of whiskey, and small quantities of coffee, sugar, and salt. This was only forty days' rations, though, and after that the men had to hunt or eat portable soup.

When the Corps departed, according to Clark, the men were in "high spirits." They

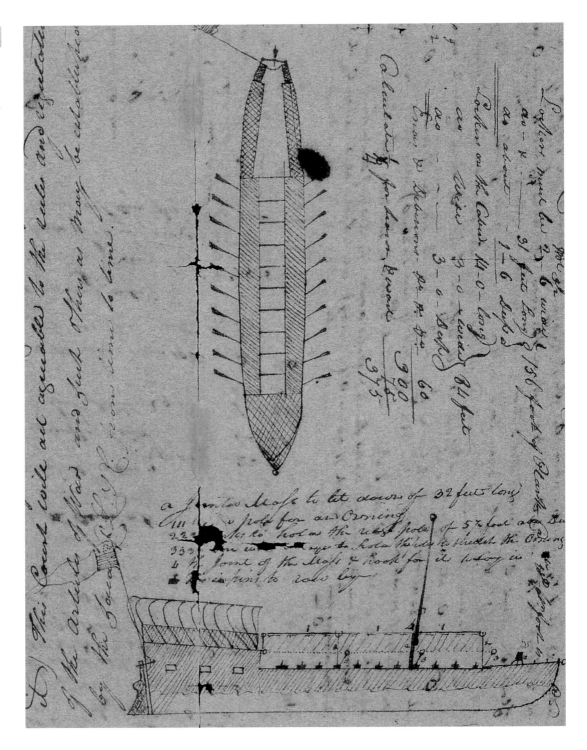

These two sketches by William Clark show the expedition's keelboat after it was modified at Camp Dubois. The overhead view clearly shows the storage lockers that lined both sides of the boat and the oars by which the men rowed it. The side view also shows the mast that was added but rarely used. Most of the time the men rowed the boat or pulled it with tow ropes.

needed that optimism in the first few months as they adjusted to life on the river.

The work was exhausting. That far south, the Missouri was an immense and powerful river, full of snags and sandbars, and the men were working against the current. At times they could raise a sail on the keelboat, but most of the time they had to row or pole themselves upstream, and in particularly bad stretches they went ashore and simply towed the boat. Most

days they traveled only ten to fourteen miles (16 to 22.5km), and sometimes only half that. Some days they seemed to make no progress at all. Ten days out, for example, the Missouri won a round when the keelboat struck a sandbar near the middle of the river. "The Swiftness of the Current wheeled the boat," wrote Clark, "Broke our Toe rope and was nearly over Setting the boat, all hand Jumped out on the upper Side and bore on that Side untill the

JOURNALS OF THE LEWIS AND CLARK EXPEDITION

The Lewis and Clark Expedition is one of the best documented journeys of early American history. The President's original orders to Meriwether Lewis had emphasized the necessity of carefully recording where the expedition went and what it found and specified that several copies of this record should be made in case one was lost or damaged. In keeping with those orders, both Lewis and Clark kept journals of their travels. They also ordered each of their sergeants to keep a journal and encouraged the privates to do so as well.

One of the great mysteries of the expedition, however, is how many journals there actually were in addition to the captains'. Among the Corps' four sergeants—Charles Floyd, John Ordway, Nathaniel Pryor, and Patrick Gass, who replaced Floyd when the latter died—Floyd, Ordway, and Gass all kept journals that have survived. Did Sergeant Pryor neglect his duty or has the journal he kept been lost? Among the privates, only Joseph Whitehouse kept a record that is known to have survived, though only part of it has been found. Another private, Robert Frazer, apparently kept a journal too, but it has never surfaced. That would make, at most, six journals from the enlisted men. Lewis, however, reported to the President in 1805 that seven men were keeping journals; so at least one, apparently, remains completely unaccounted for in addition to the missing journal of Private Frazer and the possible journal of Sergeant Pryor. The missing journals could still come to light, though. Part of Private Whitehouse's was found in a Philadelphia bookstore in 1966!

Lewis and Clark's journals contain much more than a written account of their travels. The captains also drew numerous pictures such as this one depicting the "Cock of the Plains."

Sand washed from under the boat and wheeled on the next bank by the time She wheeled a 3rd Time got a rope fast to her Stern and by means of swimmers was carried to shore." Clark named the spot "retragrade bend" because they were forced back two miles (3.2km) from that point.

Most days the men were up at dawn and on the river by 7 A.M. They usually went until midday, when they stopped for dinner, and then resumed their journey until early evening, when they made camp for the night. Hunters ranged out from the river in search of game every day, and one of the captains often walked abroad to investigate the land through which the Corps was passing. The rest of the men stayed with the boats. The captain on board would record direction and distance as the river twisted and turned, and would note the location of islands, streams entering the Missouri, or other landmarks. The sergeants each had a responsibility on board the keelboat. One in the bow kept watch for danger, either Indians or obstacles in the river; one amidships kept the men working, watched the sail, and reported islands or streams to the captain; and one in the stern served as helmsman. The privates bent their backs to the oars, poles, or towrope. There were breaks for refreshment during the day, but the sergeants were under orders to be sure "that not more time than is necessary shall be expended at each halt." Nor did the work stop when they landed for the night. The men still had to gather firewood, pitch their tents, collect their rations, prepare that day's supper as well as the next day's breakfast and dinner, and, if not on guard duty, try to get a good night's sleep while under assault by squadrons of mosquitoes.

Discipline was still tight, too. In the six months between Lewis and Clark's departure from Camp Dubois and their going into winter camp, they convened five courts-martial to hear nine cases involving six different members of the permanent Corps—about a quarter of the soldiers in that body. Charges included slipping out of camp to attend a dance in St. Charles, sleeping or drinking on guard duty, desertion,

Though the Missouri is nearly a mile wide in many places, the boats generally hugged the shore, where the slower current made it easier to row or pull the boats upstream.

October 13, 1804. *The Prisoner plead not guil[t]y to the charge exhibited against him. The court after having duly considered the evidence aduced, as well as the defense of the said prisoner, are unanimously of opinion that the prisoner John Newman is guilty of every part of the charge exhibited against him, and do sentnce him agreebly to the rules and articles of war, to receive seventy five lashes on his bear back, and to be henceforth discarded from the perminent party engaged for North Western discovery; two thirds of the Court concurring in the sum and nature of the punishment awarded. the commanding officers approve and confirm the sentence of the court, and direct the punishment take place tomorrow.*

William Clark

Years after the Lewis and Clark Expedition, the artist George Catlin paid his own tribute to Charles Floyd—the only member of the expedition to die en route. In 1832 Catlin painted the hill near Sioux City, Iowa, on which Floyd was buried. Twenty-five years later the grave was moved to protect it from erosion by the river. Today it is marked by a large monument.

and mutiny. In most cases the punishment was a whipping of between fifty and five hundred lashes. In John Newman's case, however, conviction for "having uttered repeated expressions of a highly criminal and mutinous nature" was followed by seventy-five lashes and dismissal from the permanent Corps.

Even when things went right the days were long and hard, and often things went wrong. Rain or boating accidents sometimes wet the supplies, which then had to be opened and dried to prevent spoilage. The keelboat's mast broke when its crew tried to sail under a tree hanging too low over the water. Hunters were sometimes unable to get back before dark and had to spend the night alone. George Shannon held the record for this; he spent two weeks lost—he was heading upstream in search of his companions when they were actually behind him trying to catch up. Having shot all his bullets, Shannon lived for twelve days on wild grapes and a single rabbit he managed to kill by firing a stick out of his gun at it. Tired and hungry, he finally just sat down on the riverbank in the hope that a passing trader might find him, and there the expedition found him before, as Clark wrote, he "Starved to death in a land of Plenty for the Want of Bulletes."

One man did die. Charles Floyd, one of the first men to join Lewis and Clark as they descended the Ohio and one of their sergeants as they ascended the Missouri, suddenly took ill in August as the Corps made its way north in what is now Iowa. Clark wrote that Floyd had "Beliose Chorlick" and the captains did what they could to relieve him. There was nothing either Lewis or Clark could do, though. Floyd's appendix had probably burst, and he was quickly dying of peritonitis, which doctors then had not even identified. All any doctor of that era could do was try to make the patient comfortable, and the captains did what they could. Clark stayed up all night with Floyd and the next day was preparing a warm bath for the sergeant, "hopeing it would brace him a little," when Floyd died. He was buried with "the Honors of War" and a tribute from Captain Clark: "This man at all times gave us proofs of his firmness and Deturmined resolution to do Service to his Countery and honor to himself."

New Worlds to See

The voyage upstream was more than work, discipline, and death. There were also new worlds to see. As the Corps of Discovery toiled up the Missouri, its members began to notice changes in the land and animals around them. The men of the Lewis and Clark Expedition were among the first white Americans ever to see the Great Plains, and they liked what they saw. Writing from just beyond modern Kansas City, Clark captured the awe with which he and his companions first saw the Plains:

> The Plains of this countrey are covered
> with a Leek Green Grass, well calculated
> for the sweetest and most norushing hay—
> interspersed with Cops of trees, Spreding
> ther lofty branchs over Pools Springs or
> Brooks of fine water. Groops of Shrubs
> covered with the most delicious froot is to be
> seen in every direction, and nature appears

Indian negotiations were almost as important as exploration to Lewis and Clark. Two important elements of Indian diplomatic etiquette were smoking and gift giving. Among the gifts Lewis and Clark carried were medallions such as this one, which they usually presented only to men they took to be tribal leaders.

to have exerted herself to butify the Senery by the variety of flours Delicately and highly flavered raised above the Grass, which Strikes & profumes the Sensation, and amuses the mind throws it into Conjecturing the cause of So magnificent a Senery...in a Country thus Situated far removed from the Sivilised world.

And there were Indians. One of the tasks that Jefferson assigned the expedition was to meet and negotiate with the Indian peoples it encountered. The captains took this responsibility very seriously. As they sailed upstream into Indian territory, they began sending men out to look for natives with whom they could negotiate. But summer was the time for hunting buffalo, and the scouts had a hard time finding anyone for their captains to talk to. They finally made contact in late July, and August saw several peaceful—though not very productive—meetings between Lewis and Clark and the Oto and Missouri Indians as well as the Yankton Sioux.

On each of these occasions the American captains put on their dress uniforms, hoisted the American flag, paraded their men, and tried to provide as much ceremony as they could under the circumstances. They exchanged gifts—an essential part of Indian diplomatic protocol—smoked the calumet (a ceremonial native pipe), made and listened to speeches,

and tried to impress their guests with the power and sincerity of the United States. What Lewis and Clark wanted was for the different tribes of the Missouri Valley to live in peace with one another and to trade exclusively with the United States. What the natives wanted was very different. War, chiefly in the form of tribes raiding one another, was an important element in Plains Indian culture, and it is highly unlikely that the Oto, Missouri, or Yankton were interested in changing that. What they wanted was the means to wage war more effectively, especially against the better-armed Teton Sioux, who were then establishing themselves as the dominant power of the Middle Missouri Valley. It did not matter to the Oto or Yankton if the means to defend themselves came from British, Spanish, or American traders. As a result, neither side got what it wanted from these first meetings. They were generally friendly enough, though, and for the Americans at least, they provided an opportunity to relax a little and glimpse Plains Indian culture.

The same could not be said of Lewis and Clark's initial encounter with the Teton Sioux. The captains knew they must deal with the Tetons but did not relish the idea. In the early nineteenth century, the Teton Sioux lived on either side of the Missouri in present-day South Dakota and often used their position and power to control trade between tribes farther upstream and traders from St. Louis. They simply stopped smaller, less well armed parties or allowed them to pass only after they paid tribute. President Jefferson was aware of this and, in one of his last letters to Lewis before the Corps' departure, had urged him to pay special attention to the Teton Sioux "because of their immense power."

Several meetings took place in late September near and in a Teton village that Sergeant Ordway estimated had nearly a thousand residents. For four days the two sides talked, exchanged gifts, socialized, demonstrated their power, and tried to intimidate each other. The Tetons wanted to stop Lewis and Clark from dealing directly with the tribes upstream or at least force them to acknowledge that they would do so only with Teton approval. The Americans were determined to show they could go where they liked. In the end, neither side was willing to use force, but they came close. Twice over the four days soldiers and warriors faced off with loaded weapons and hurled insults at one another as Tetons grabbed a line from one of the Corps' boats and insisted that it stay. Only when Lewis and Clark provided additional, though small, presents did the stalemate end. The encounter did nothing to advance American aims and convinced Lewis and Clark that nothing but greater economic or military power would force the Sioux to back down. "These are the vilest miscreants of the savage race," Clark wrote in his journal. "Unless these people are reduced to order, by coercive measures, I am ready to pronounce that the citizens of the United States can never enjoy but partially the advantages which the Missouri presents."

By now, it was nearly October. For another month the Corps worked its way up the Missouri before the captains decided it was time to stop. On October 31 Lewis wrote: "The river being very low and the season so far advanced that it frequently shuts up with ice in this climate we determined to spend the winter in this neighbourhood." They were then in Mandan country, what is now central North Dakota, and there they stayed until the following spring.

Natives, too, did their best to impress visiting dignitaries. Among some tribes, including these Teton Sioux painted by George Catlin, one of the great honors paid important visitors was a feast of dog. According to John Ordway, when Lewis and Clark met the Teton Sioux the Indians "killed Several dogs and cooked them in a decent manner to treat our people with."

Chapter Four

Mandan Winter

TO SOME OF THE MEN WITH LEWIS AND CLARK that winter, the Mandan villages must have seemed remote beyond belief; they were sixteen hundred miles (2,574km) from St. Louis and as far west as any Americans had ever traveled overland from the United States. To those who knew or lived in the West, though, Mandan country was a cultural and economic crossroads, which is why Lewis and Clark had planned from the start to winter there.

The Mandan and Hidatsa Peoples

The Mandan were a settled, agricultural people living in two villages near the junction of the Knife and Missouri Rivers, in what is now central North Dakota. Each of the towns Lewis

NORTH DAKOTA

● Fort Mandan

Yellowstone River

Missouri River

MONTANA

Powder River

SOUTH DAKOTA

PAGE 50: *Mandan homes, such as these reconstructed in North Dakota, were perfectly suited to the harsh winters of the northern Plains. Thick walls of dirt and sod provided insulation, and the tunnel-like doorway acted as an airlock to keep out cold air.* ABOVE: *Lewis and Clark spent the winter of 1804-1805 very comfortably at a fort they built among the Mandan people.*

and Clark visited contained forty to fifty lodges and some six hundred residents, but these were just the remnants of a much larger Mandan community that had shrunk dramatically in the late eighteenth century as a result of smallpox and Sioux expansion. The towns were among the most distinctive of any on the northern Plains. Situated on bluffs above the river, they were generally circular and surrounded by a palisade and dry moat. Each contained a plaza in which residents erected a cedar post representing Lone Man, the legendary Mandan who saved his people from a great flood by building their first walled village. Around the plaza were ceremonial lodges, and beyond were dozens of hemispheric earthen lodges packed so tightly together that it was sometimes difficult to pass between them. Nearby, on the Knife River, were three more villages occupied by Hidatsa Indians, who were culturally and linguistically related to the Mandan.

Trading and Negotiating

Though declining in number and in size, the Mandan and Hidatsa villages were still central

to the economy of the northern Plains because they were the point at which several different economies converged. Mandan and Hidatsa farmers grew more corn, beans, and squash than they needed for themselves, and their surplus crops attracted nonagricultural tribes from every quarter. From the north and east came Sioux and Cree, who had contact with French and English traders in Canada. From the south and west came Cheyenne and Crow, who had access to Spanish horses from New Mexico. The result was a bazaar in which river valley farmers and Plains buffalo hunters exchanged corn, beans, meat, and hides of their own production as well as horses, mules, guns, knives, and other products originally acquired from European traders.

Such an important marketplace was immensely attractive to Lewis and Clark. Food was certainly part of the attraction. The captains needed to feed their men over the winter and resupply for the coming summer, and Mandan corn would feed American explorers just as it did Sioux hunters. The mix of peoples visiting Mandan country might also provide a larger audience for Lewis and Clark's diplomatic efforts; if they could meet leaders of several tribes at once, they might be able to negotiate more easily the sort of peace that Jefferson wanted. Finally, Lewis and Clark planned to further their education among the Mandan. The maps with which they traveled that first summer ended at the Mandan villages, and the captains planned to use their time that winter talking to the Mandan and to the other visitors in an effort to learn as much as they could about the lands farther west before trying to cross them.

On arriving among the Mandan, Lewis and Clark first paid visits to each of the Mandan villages and then held a council to which they invited both Mandan and Hidatsa leaders. As they had done before, the Americans urged their native guests to accept American sovereignty, make peace with their neighbors, and trade only with Americans. But in a new twist, the captains tried to encourage

LEFT: *In Lewis and Clark's day, the Mandan lived in two villages on the Missouri, like this one painted later by George Catlin. Catlin depicted the circular lodges around a central plaza that was typical of Mandan villages and in the center of the plaza the wooden enclosure surrounding a cedar post that represented Lone Man.* BELOW: *This view of the Knife River shows clearly the river bluffs on which the Mandan and Hidatsa chose to build their villages. Bottomland between the bluffs and the river provided fertile land for crops; villages sat safely above the flood plain, and villagers could watch the river for arriving friends or enemies.*

THE MANDAN WORLD

The Mandan lived in a world of villages. Though most white Americans, including Lewis and Clark, generally thought of Indians in terms of tribes or nations like their own, Mandan life was much less centralized than that. Ties of language and culture did create a wider Mandan identity, but life revolved around individual villages.

Their villages generally stood on bluffs at the edge of the Missouri River's flood plain. Before the Missouri was dammed in the twentieth century, it flooded every spring across a wide river bottom. The Mandan built their villages just above this flood zone: close enough to exploit the fertile soil left by centuries of flooding but safely above the water's reach. Below the villages, Mandan women grew the corn, beans, squash, and sunflowers that provided much of their families' food. The rest of

their food, plus skins for their clothing and bone for tools, came from buffalo and other game killed by the men during regular hunting expeditions onto the Great Plains. Villages were also the center of social and political life. Each had its own Okipa lodge, the center of ceremonial life; its own set of the thirteen clans into which Mandans divided their population; and its own set of two chiefs: a peace chief and a war chief, one for each situation.

By the time Lewis and Clark arrived, disease and pressure from the better-armed Teton Sioux had reduced the number of Mandan villages from a dozen or more to two. Mandan culture, however, remained intact and impressed Lewis and Clark mightily. "They are brave, humane, and hospitable," wrote Clark, who also called them "the most friendly, well disposed Indians inhabiting the Missouri."

George Catlin painted this Mandan rainmaking ceremony when he visited the tribe during the 1830s.

peace more directly. They had brought with them a village chief of the Arikara tribe, which lived downstream from the Mandan and was currently at war with them. Earlier in October Lewis and Clark had tried to convince the Arikara to stop their feud with the Mandan and Hidatsa, and they brought this chief to be an Arikara spokesman to the Mandan and Hidatsa. After the speechmaking, pipe smoking, and gift giving, the council broke up and Lewis and Clark waited while each of the Indian villages discussed the idea of peace. They waited all winter. The Mandan made some vague promises about wanting peace but did little to show they meant it; the Hidatsa said and did nothing. When Lewis and Clark left the following spring, little had changed in Mandan or Hidatsa foreign affairs.

Though farming was the Mandans' chief source of food, they also hunted buffalo. This 1844 lithograph by George Catlin shows one of their techniques. A circle of mounted hunters surrounded the buffalo and, on a signal, began riding around the herd in an ever-smaller circle until they trapped and killed a number of the animals.

Fort Mandan

Diplomacy aside, Lewis and Clark spent a very successful winter among the Mandan. Once the grand council was over, the first order of business was housing for the Americans. After several days of looking at possible sites for a winter camp, the captains selected one in a wooded bottom several miles downstream from the Mandan villages. There the men set to work building Fort Mandan—"we called it Fort Mandan, in honour of our friendly neighbours," Lewis wrote his mother. Construction began in early November under the supervision of dozens of curious Mandan and Hidatsa. Building was sometimes slowed by bitter cold (-43°F [-41°C] one morning) that required the men to work in shifts and relieve one another every hour, so they did not finish until just before Christmas.

The fort was triangular. Rows of living quarters, including separate "huts" for the captains, formed two of its sides, while the third was a stockade wall eighteen feet (5.5m) high. The wall was pierced by a single gate, and opposite the gate, where the rows of cabins met, were several storage rooms with a sentry's post on top. All the living quarters were built of cottonwood logs, roofed with split logs known as puncheons, and at least some of them had stone chimneys and puncheon floors. They were, wrote Sergeant Ordway, "warm and comfortable."

Once construction of the fort was well in hand, fully half the men spent part of December hunting buffalo with the Indians. The Corps planned to live on fresh meat as much as possible that winter and husband its supply of pork, corn, and other preserved food for the coming journey, so it was essential that they bring in as much meat as they could. For five days, in temperatures often below zero (-18°C) and never above freezing with snow nearly a foot (30.5cm) deep, the men killed and butchered buffalo and packed the meat on horses for transport back to Fort Mandan. This fed them until early February, when Clark and

half the men went out to replenish the supply. It had been weeks since any buffalo had been seen around the fort, so the hunters went sixty miles (96.5km) down the Missouri, walking on the ice in search of game. "We killed 40 deer, 3 Bulls [and] 19 Elk," reported Clark, "maney So meager that they were unfit for use." Despite Clark's disappointment, he and the others did manage to bring back more than a ton (908kg) of meat, which saw the Americans through the rest of the winter.

One preparation for the season somehow escaped the attention of Lewis and Clark: they neglected to haul their boats out of the river before winter set in. Leaving the boats in the water not only exposed them to the crushing pressure of ice as the river froze but also left them vulnerable to heavy blows from shifting ice once the river began to break up in the spring. Perhaps the captains were too busy building and hunting, but the complete silence in their journals about the matter as winter approached, combined with Jefferson's earlier claim to Congress that the Missouri would provide ice-free access to the western fur trade, suggests that these Virginians, who had never lived through a North Dakota winter, had no idea how rough it would be.

By late January they knew they had made a mistake, and by February it worried them. "The situation of our boat and perogues is now allarming," Lewis confessed. "They are firmly

York, William Clark's slave, was often a source of fascination among Indians the expedition encountered. Most had never seen "a black white man" and some, such as the Hidatsa shown in this painting by Charles M. Russell, tried to rub York's color off.

Mandan Winter

57

which are seperated by streams of water.
this peculiarly unfortunate because so soon
as we cut through the first strata of ice the
water rushes up and rises as high as the upper surface of the ice and thus creates such
a debth of water as ~~has~~ renders it impracti=
=cable to cut away the lower strata ~~p~~ which appears
firmly attatched to, and confining the bottom
of the vessels. the instruments we have hither
=to used has been the ax only, with which, we
have made several attempts ~~that~~ proved un-
=successfull from the cause above mentioned.
we then determined to attempt freeing them from
the ice by means of boiling water which we
purposed heating in the vessels by means of
hot stones, but this expedient proved also fruit
=less, as every species of stone which we could
procure in the neighbourhood partook so
much of the calcarious genus that they burst
into small particles on being exposed to the
heat of the fire. we now determined as the
dernier resort to prepare a parsel of
Iron spikes and attatch them to the end of
small poles of convenient length and endeavour
by means of them to free the vessels from the ice.

inclosed in the Ice and almost covered with snow." Cutting them out with axes failed because the ice was in layers with water in between, and "so soon as we cut through the first strata of ice the water rushes up...and thus creates such a debth of water as renders it impracticable to cut away the lower strata." Next they poured water into the boats and tried to heat it by dropping in hot rocks. Unfortunately, the rocks "burst into small particles on being exposed to the heat of the fire," and this plan was no more successful than the axes had been. As a last resort, wrote Clark, "we had all the Iron we Could get & Some axes put on long poles and picked throught the ice, under the first water, which was not more than 6 or 8 inches [15 or 20cm] deep." Then they hauled the boats ashore. It took four days altogether, "with great Dificuelty & trouble," but it was done by late February.

Exploration and Discovery

Crises such as this were rare. In general, the winter at Fort Mandan was both relaxing and productive for red and white Americans alike. It was certainly an opportunity for the two groups to socialize. Almost every day Mandan or Hidatsa visitors came to the fort. They had certainly seen white men before—there were several living in their midst at the time—but never in such large numbers or in anything as close as Fort Mandan was to the white man's "natural environment." There was new technology to see, such as the keelboat and the blacksmith's bellows, and countless examples of the strangers' alien customs and etiquette. There was also a man who could dance while standing on his hands, as well as a black man, which the natives had never seen and to whom they ascribed "great medison." To the Indians around Fort Mandan, the Lewis and Clark Expedition was a sort of traveling circus.

To the men of the expedition, of course, the Mandan and Hidatsa villages were just as mysterious. Many of Lewis and Clark's men spent hours exploring the native community. Though cultural and linguistic barriers often kept them from fully understanding what they saw, members of the expedition watched Indian games, visited Indian lodges, had sex with Indian women, and were even invited to participate in at least one Mandan ceremony. To attract buffalo and to pass the hunting prowess of older, more skilled hunters on to younger ones, the Mandan held a ceremony in which young men offered their wives to older men. If the older men had sex with the women, the act would transmit the men's knowledge and skill to the women, who could then transfer it to their husbands through sex with them. Clark described this ceremony in his journal, though he did not understand the ritual involved, and then wrote, "we sent a man to this Medisan Dance last night, [and] they gave him 4 girls." There was no report from the man.

The Corps also went into business and found a way of increasing its food supply for the coming journey. In December they erected a blacksmith shop that was soon doing a booming business sharpening and repairing axes, hoes, and other metal implements for their Indian owners, who paid for this service with corn. When everything worn or broken had been repaired, the smiths went to work manufacturing battle-axes of a type to which the Indians were "pecurly attached." In Clark's view the weapon was "very inconvenient" and not especially effective, but the demand for them was great, and they were "the only means by which we procure Corn."

The captains were also busy that winter. They already had an enormous amount of information for President Jefferson and spent many days copying and amplifying their journals for him. They produced a detailed description of the rivers and creeks they had seen and of the land around them. They organized their impressions of the Indians they had met under nineteen different categories, ranging from "the Sounds by which the Inds express the Names of their respective Nations" to "the Kind of pel-

OPPOSITE: *Merriwether Lewis' journal entry for February 3, 1805, describes the Corps' efforts to free their boats from the frozen Missouri River. Attacking the ice with axes had failed, as had trying to melt it by heating water inside the boats. "As the denier resort," Lewis planned an assault using iron spikes attached to the ends of wooden poles.*

tries & Robes which they Annually supply or furnish." Clark drafted a large map of the route they had taken thus far. The charts with which Lewis and Clark left Camp Dubois had shown quite accurately the Lower Missouri and the Mandan villages, but in between there was only a dotted line tracing the conjectural route of the Missouri. Working with the notes they had taken earlier of the distance and direction traveled each day, Clark now prepared the most accurate map in existence of the Middle Missouri River.

However, Lewis and Clark were not content simply to pass on what they already knew. They spent a great deal of time and energy collecting new information, especially about what lay before them. Hidatsa war parties often traveled west toward the Rockies to raid the Shoshone and thus knew firsthand much of the Missouri River Valley above Fort Mandan. From these raids, the Hidatsa sometimes brought

back captives, and these adopted members of the tribe often knew parts of the land even farther west. Tribes that visited the Mandan or Hidatsa to trade also told stories about regions to the north and west. Getting this information required great patience. Neither Lewis nor Clark spoke any language but English, which none of the Indians spoke. Asking a Hidatsa warrior about the Upper Missouri meant first translating the question into French through one of the métis members of the Corps, then from French to Hidatsa through one of the French or métis traders living with them. Anything directed at a Shoshone, Arikara, or Assiniboine, meant further translation, and every answer followed the same steps in reverse.

Two of the key links in this chain of bilingual informants were Toussaint Charbonneau and his Indian wife, Sacagawea. Charbonneau was a French-Canadian trader living among the Hidatsa when Lewis and Clark arrived. Earlier that year he had purchased from the Hidatsa a young Shoshone woman, perhaps sixteen years old, who had been captured several years earlier at the Three Forks of the Missouri. She was now one of his wives and was known by the name Sacagawea. Soon after Lewis and Clark arrived among the Mandan, they hired Charbonneau as an interpreter, and through the winter he served in that capacity. Sacagawea provided an unexpected bonus; she had been old enough before her capture to understand where the Shoshone traveled west of the Three Forks and now passed that information, through Charbonneau, to Lewis and Clark.

Leaving Fort Mandan

Early in March the Corps began to prepare for its departure from Fort Mandan. As the weather grew milder, the men lay their equipment and supplies in the sun to air out and dry prior to repacking them. They recaulked the keelboat and pirogues and, because the keelboat was returning to St. Louis, built six canoes to replace it on the journey upstream. They were in "high spirits," wrote Clark, and ready to go. The captains finished their maps and reports to the president, packed several boxes of specimens to send him, chose men to replace Moses Reed and John Newman, who had been discharged from the Permanent Detachment for

insubordination or desertion, and made final plans for the coming year. By late March the ice was breaking up, and it was almost time to continue on their way.

On April 7, 1805, Lewis wrote a final letter to the president from Fort Mandan. It was not quite as optimistic as one written a week earlier to his mother, in which Lewis claimed that it was less than half a day's march between navigable waters on the Missouri and those of the Columbia. Lewis was more realistic with Jefferson, but still confident: "At this moment, every individual of the party are in good health and excellent spirits; zealously attached to the enterprise, and anxious to proceed."

They had plenty of food and, he thought, reliable information about the route ahead. That far north the river was less powerful, so Lewis expected the Corps to move more quickly than it had farther south. He predicted that they would reach the Pacific early enough in the season to return at least as far as the Upper Missouri, if not to Fort Mandan, by the coming winter and promised to meet Jefferson at Monticello in September 1806. "I can foresee no material or probable obstruction to our progress, and entertain therefore the most sanguine hopes of complete success." The imminent challenges that Lewis could not foresee on that warm April morning were grizzly bears, the portage around the Falls of the Missouri, and the Lolo Trail.

During the winter at Fort Mandan, John Shields and Alexander Willard, the Corps of Discovery's blacksmiths, made dozens of axes like this one drawn by William Clark. Initially, Lewis and Clark traded them to the Mandan and Hidatsa for corn. From there, however, the axes entered a native trading system that stretched beyond the Rockies. A year later, as the Corps crossed Idaho on the way back from the Pacific, John Ordway found Nez Perce Indians gambling with axes made at Fort Mandan.

Chapter Five

Into the Unknown

SOON AFTER LEWIS FINISHED HIS LETTER TO THE president, two small flotillas pushed into the river at Fort Mandan and set off in opposite directions: the pirogues and six canoes headed upstream, while the keelboat and a canoe went downstream. In the eight boats heading upstream, bound for the Pacific, were Lewis and Clark; twenty-six other soldiers; Clark's slave, York; two civilian interpreters, George Drouillard and Toussaint Charbonneau; Charbonneau's wife, Sacagawea; and the couple's infant son. On the keelboat were seven or eight soldiers carrying back the reports and specimens collected so far by Lewis and Clark.

No doubt, some of the men heading south were looking forward to their arrival in St. Louis, but not John Newman. Private Newman had originally been chosen to go to the

On the map:

Milk River

Great Falls ●

MONTANA

Three Forks ●

Yellowstone River

Tongue River

Powder River

NORTH DAKOTA

● Fort Mandan

Missouri River

WYOMING

SOUTH DAKOTA

---

*the water is yet very could, and so frequent
are those point that they are one fourth of
their time in the water, added to this the
banks and bluffs along which they are
obliged to pass [when towing the boats] are
so slippery and the mud so tenacious that
they are unable to wear their mockersons,
and in that situation draging the heavy
burthen of a canoe and walking ocasional-
ly for several hundred yards over the sharp
fragments of rocks which tumble from the
clifts...; in short their labour is incredibly
painfull and great, yet those fellows bear it
without a murmur.*

In spite of the hard labor, the men's journals for this period convey an air of adventure
and a sense of joy. They were now traveling
twenty miles (32km) a day, nearly double their
average from the preceding spring. The weather was turning fine; there were still some frosty
mornings and flurries of snow, but there were
also days so warm that the men worked nearly
naked. And the food was great. Ordway wrote
that "the Game is gitting so pleanty and tame
in this country that Some of the party clubbed
them out of their way." There were beaver,
deer, elk, and antelope, but mainly there were
buffalo. The Corps was now in the heart of
buffalo country, and Charbonneau revealed his
true calling: Lewis called him "our wrighthand
cook." Lewis was so taken with Charbonneau's
boudin blanc—a buffalo sausage—that he paid
it a glowing tribute in his journal, carefully
describing how it was made and proclaiming it
"one of the great delacies of the forrest."

This leg of the journey also brought the
Americans some exciting lessons in one of the
great dangers of the forest: the grizzly bear.
They had heard stories of these great beasts
from the Mandan but clearly considered them
exaggerated. Three weeks out from Fort
Mandan, Lewis and one of the hunters had
their first encounter with a grizzly. An adoles-
cent male charged Lewis after the hunter had
wounded the animal, but Lewis killed the bear
before it reached him. This simply confirmed

PAGE 62: *As the explorers
traveled through territory
unknown to any other
white men, they saw flora
and fauna that no
European had encoun-
tered before. The Corps
painstakingly recorded
their observations for pos-
terity and for their own
knowledge.* ABOVE: *From
Fort Mandan to Three
Forks was one of the most
pleasant sections of Lewis
and Clark's journey. No
whites had ever traveled
this portion of the
Missouri River, which
often seemed a paradise to
the American explorers.*

Pacific but had been expelled from the party
for insubordination in October 1804. He spent
the winter at Fort Mandan trying to prove that
he was worthy of reinstatement, as we know
from Lewis and Clark's reports, but failed. Now
he had to watch as his former companions
slowly paddled north. Neither he nor they
knew what lay ahead; they were heading into
country where no white man had ever been.
But John Newman did know that he was missing out on the trip of a lifetime.

After Fort Mandan

The next two months, which were spent traveling from Fort Mandan to the Falls of the
Missouri, were probably the most enjoyable
period of the expedition. The days were still
long, though, and the work was still hard.
Lewis captured that vividly in a journal entry
from late May:

> *The obstructions of rocky points and
> riffles [in the river] still continue as yester-
> day; at those places the men are compelled
> to be in the water even to their armpits, and*

Lewis' belief that the Mandan had exaggerated the grizzly's prowess. He conceded that the species was more aggressive than the familiar black bear but not dangerously so. "The Indians may well fear this anamal equiped as they generally are with their bows and arrows or indifferent fuzees," concluded Lewis, "but in the hands of skillfull riflemen they are by no means as formidable or dangerous as they have been represented."

His opinion soon changed. One week later the Corps killed its first adult grizzly. Clark and Drouillard shot this "large and turrible looking animal" ten times before killing it, and Clark pronounced it "the largest [animal] of the Carnivorous kind I ever saw." Lewis not only described the bear in great detail, but also its effect on the men. "I find that the curiossity of our party is pretty well satisfyed with rispect to this anamal," he declared. "The difficulty with which they die when even shot through the vital parts has staggered the resolution [of] several of them, others however seem keen for action with the bear." If Lewis was still one of those keen for action, his interest faded a few days later when he helped dispatch yet another grizzly. "These bear being so hard to die reather intimedates us all," he wrote. "I must confess that I do not like the gentlemen and had reather fight two Indians than one bear."

Choosing the Right River

Rapids and bears notwithstanding, Lewis and Clark's first great challenge since leaving Fort Mandan came only when they reached what they later called Marias River in what is now north central Montana. Until that point, the geographic information provided by Indian informants among the Mandan had been wonderfully accurate. The Yellowstone and Milk Rivers had been right where the Americans expected them to be, so at their mouths there had been no question which way to go. Marias River, however, was not supposed to be there. According to the Indians, no river entered the Missouri in this vicinity, and because the Marias was so close in appearance and size to the Missouri, it was not immediately clear which was the Missouri. A mistake now, in early June, could have been disastrous, and

This illustration from Patrick Gass' published journal shows one of Lewis and Clark's numerous encounters with grizzly bears. It also shows that the men quickly learned to put as many bullets as possible into a grizzly as fast as they could fire them. It sometimes took a dozen shots to kill an adult bear.

June 14, 1805 *I selected a fat buffaloe and shot him very well, through the lungs; while I was gazeing attentively on the poor anamal discharging blood in streams from his mouth and nostrils, expecting him to fall every instant, and having entirely forgotten to reload my rifle, a large white, or reather brown bear, had perceived and crept on me within 20 steps before I discovered him; in the first moment I drew up my gun to shoot, but at the same instant recolected that she was not loaded and that he was too near for me to hope to perform this opperation before he reached me, as he was then briskly advancing on me; it was an open level plain; . . . . in short there was no place by means of which I could conceal myself from this monster untill I could charge my rifle.*

Meriwether Lewis

Lewis and Clark knew it. As Lewis put it, "To ascend such stream to the rocky Mountain or perhaps much further before we could inform ourselves whether it did approach the Columbia or not, and then be obliged to return and take the other stream would not only loose us the whole of this season but would probably so dishearten the party that it might defeat the expedition altogether."

The captains decided to explore both branches before making their choice. Lewis took one party up the north fork, while Clark and a second party ascended the south. Each spent several days exploring and then returned to the junction to compare notes and make a decision. Sunday, June 9, was the day of their reckoning.

They considered the results of their reconnaissance, they studied the maps they had brought from Washington and St. Louis, and they went over the notes they had made at Fort Mandan. In the captains' view, everything pointed to the south fork as the true Missouri: British traders in Canada had never found a river that went very far into the Rockies, so following the north fork would probably bring Lewis and Clark to those "rivulets" the British had found and not to anything that would bring them close to the Columbia; Indians had told the Americans that the Falls of the Missouri were southwest of the Mandan country, not northwest; and the water of the south fork was clear, which fit the Indians' description of water found at the Falls.

To co-commanders Lewis and Clark, the choice was clear, but every other man in the Corps disagreed with their conclusion. Even Pierre Cruzatte, whom everyone in the expedition considered the most experienced Missouri River hand, believed the north fork was "the true genuine Missouri." Nevertheless, every man in the Corps was ready to follow their captains: according to Lewis, "they said very cheerfully that they were ready to follow us any wher we thought proper to direct but that they still thought that the other was the river."

OPPOSITE: *The first adult grizzly bear Lewis and Clark encountered was a sobering sight; it stood over seven feet (2.1m) tall, weighed five or six hundred pounds (225 to 275kg), and took ten bullets to kill. "It was a most tremendious looking animal," wrote Meriwether Lewis.* PAGE 68: *Clark's map of the Falls and the Portage of the Missouri shows that the Falls were actually a series of falls and rapids extending miles along the river. The portage route, shown by a dotted line on the left-hand side of the map, left the Missouri below the Falls and rejoined it above them, after crossing almost twenty miles (33km) of rocky, cactus-strewn desert.*

With every man convinced they were wrong, and finding the men "so determined in this belief," Lewis and Clark decided on a compromise of sorts. They would take the south fork, but Lewis and a small party would hurry ahead by land and search for the Falls or some other confirmation that they were on the right course while Clark, who was better with boats than Lewis was, came along by water. In this way, explained Lewis, "if we were in an error...[we would] be able to detect it and rectify it as soon as possible." If anyone still had reservations, they hid them well. No journal mentions any grumbling after the decision was made, and Ordway wrote that in the evening before they set out on the south fork the men "had a frolick fiddled & danced & sang untill late in the evening."

The captains were right. The south fork was the main branch of the Missouri, and it did not take long to confirm. Lewis and four others went ahead on June 11 and rejoined the main party just five days later with word that they had found a series of five cataracts ahead—the Great Falls of the Missouri. Finding the Falls was no doubt a great relief to every member of the Corps. But relief must have quickly given way to concern because now they had to find a way around the falls. These were not the sort of rapids they had overcome earlier by getting into the water and pulling the boats along. Some of these were fifty-foot (15m)-high waterfalls—higher and more powerful than any either Lewis or Clark had ever seen before. The only option was to carry the boats and equipment around them, and that portage was the greatest ordeal the expedition had yet faced.

Portage Around the Falls

The expedition, traveling upstream, established a base camp at the lower end of the falls from which to organize the portage. While Clark sought a route around the falls, Lewis directed the men to construct four sets of wheels from trees on which to haul the canoes and baggage. He also had them prepare an underground cache of food and supplies for their return trip, hide the remaining pirouge (they had already left one pirouge and a cache of supplies at the junction of the Missouri and Marias Rivers for their return trip), and scrape elk skins for the exterior of the iron boat—the frame brought from Harper's Ferry for assembly above the Falls. Every day Lewis grew more concerned. From the information obtained at Fort Mandan, they had expected a relatively short portage, and Clark was taking longer than he should have. "I am apprehensive from his stay that the portage is longer than we had calculated on."

When Clark did finally return, he confirmed Lewis' fears. Starting from the river above the falls, Clark had traveled overland to the camp below the falls, marking the route with stakes so that men traversing the portage would not get lost. He was forced to detour farther away from the river than he wanted because he had to bypass a deep ravine. This made the route fairly level, which was Clark's prime concern, but just over eighteen miles (29km) long.

Transporting the boats and baggage began on June 22 and involved five trips over eleven grueling days. Though afternoon temperatures never got out of the seventies (above 26°C), it was hot work, and because the portage route went around the ravines there was no water along the route except rainwater, which the men drank from puddles. The soil was not soft dirt, like a Virginia forest or meadow; it consisted of small, sharp stones and was often covered with prickly pear—low, spreading cactus with strong, sharp thorns. After the first day

At the junction of the Missouri (upper right) and Marias (upper left) Rivers the expedition faced the greatest dilemma in its first thirteen months of travel. Which stream was "the true genuine Missouri"? A mistake here could have been fatal, so the expedition spent several days scouting the two rivers before making a decision.

the men put double soles in their moccasins, but they still suffered bruised and punctured feet. Axles or tongues on the wheels broke three times and had to be repaired.

Thunderstorms one afternoon forced the men to take cover from hail the size of eggs, and the rain that fell rendered parts of the portage impassable. With good reason, Ordway wrote when it was over that the men "rejoiced that we have got through Such a laborious & fatiguing portage."

The Iron Boat

Lewis, meanwhile, remained at the upper end of the portage with a small contingent of boat-builders. It was time to assemble the iron boat and justify both the effort that Lewis put into it at Harper's Ferry and that of the Corps in transporting it some three thousand miles (4,800km). It is clear from Lewis' journal entries that he placed great importance on the success of this experiment—far more than the boat merited simply as a means of transportation. It

was Lewis' "favorite boat," and it was the only one he called "she." Now, he wrote, "my constant attention was necessary to every part of the work." Elk and buffalo skins were cleaned and stitched together for the exterior; wood was collected and fashioned into cross braces; and bark was stripped to line the craft's interior. Soon Lewis could boast that "her form is as complete as I could wish it."

All that was missing was tar. Lewis had planned to use tar or pitch to seal the boat, but none of the trees at the Falls was resinous. He grew increasingly distressed as this became clear, because without tar, he admitted, "I fear the whole operation of my boat will be useless." The best he could do was coat it with a mixture of tallow, charcoal, and beeswax, which he thought made the boat look better even if it did nothing to make it watertight.

Lewis' proudest moment must have been the boat's launch, when "she lay like a perfect cork on the water." It soon became clear, however, that his fears had been justified. Within hours the boat began to leak badly, and Lewis knew that he could ill afford to spend more

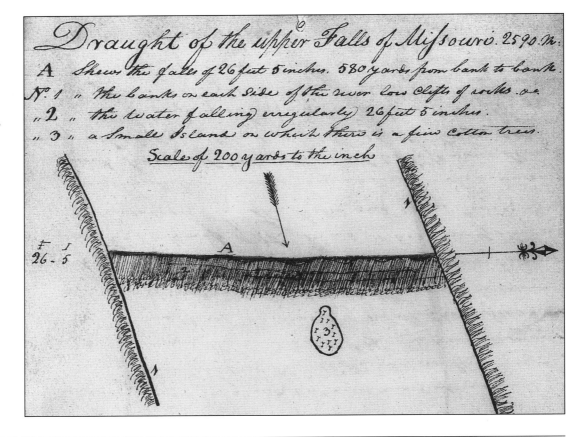

Into the Unknown

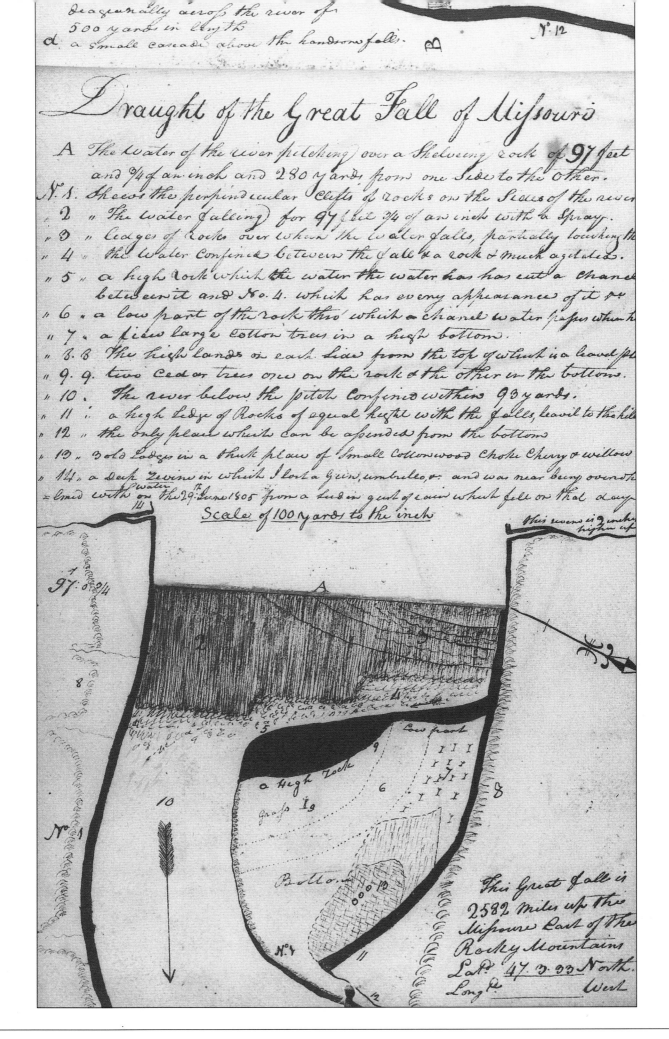

deaugonally across the river of
500 yards in length
d. a small cascade above the handrow falls.   B   N. 12

Draught of the Great Fall of Missouri

A The water of the river pitching over a shelveing rock of **97** feet
and 3/4 of an inch and 280 yards, from one side to the other.
N. 1. shews the perpindicular clifts of rocks on the sides of the river
" 2 " The water falling for 97 feet 3/4 of an inch with a spray.
" 3 " ledges of rocks over which the water falls, partially toucheng the
" 4 " the water confined between the fall & a rock & much agitated.
" 5 " a high rock which the water the water has has cut a chanel
       between it and No. 4. which has every appearance of it or
" 6 " a low part of the rock thro' which a chanel water passes when h
" 7 " a few large cotton trees in a high bottom.
" 8. 8 the high lands on each side from the top of which is a level pl
" 9. 9 two cedar trees one on the rock & the other in the bottom.
" 10 . The river below the pitch confined within 93 yards.
" 11 . a high ledge of rocks of equal heght with the falls, leavil to the hil
" 12 " the only place which can be asended from the bottom
" 13 . 3 old lodges in a thick place of small cottonwood choke cherry & willow
" 14 . a deep revine in which I lost a gun, umbrello, &. and was near being over wh
= lmed with water on the 29th June 1805 from a sudin gust of rain which fell on that day

Scale of 100 yards to the inch

This Great Fall is
2582 miles up the
Missouri East of the
Rocky Mountains
Lat. 47. 3. 03 North.
Longde ——— West

time trying to fix her. "I therefore relinquished all further hope of my favorite boat and ordered her to be sunk in the water that the skins might become soft in order to better take her in peices tomorrow and deposite the iron fraim at this place as it could probably be of no further service to us." While Lewis attended to his boat's burial the next day, Clark took a party to a wooded bottom upstream to start building two more canoes. Life went on, and the Corps of Discovery had to keep moving.

Looking for the Shoshone

By mid-July the Falls were behind them, and it was time to start thinking about the next challenge: finding and negotiating with the Shoshone Indians. Shoshone cooperation would be essential if Lewis and Clark were to cross from the Missouri to the Columbia as they planned. Not only did the Americans have no idea which route to take through the Rockies, but without Shoshone horses the men

would never be able to carry enough food and equipment to make the trip. The Corps' success, and perhaps survival, depended on finding the Shoshone and convincing them to provide horses and guides.

Lewis and Clark certainly understood this and had already been thinking about it. Leaving Fort Mandan, they had assumed that Sacagawea, herself a Shoshone, would help them in the negotiations with her people. They had a bad scare, though, when Sacagawea fell ill that spring and reminded them just how fragile their plans were. When Lewis learned how sick she was, he wrote in his journal that he was concerned for her sake as well as that of the expedition "from the consideration of her being our only dependence for a friendly negociation with the Snake [Shoshone] Indians on whom we depend for horses to assist us in our portage from the Missouri to the columbia River." Just four days later he and Clark made a change in their plans that seems to reflect a new realization that Sacagawea might not be there to assist them. Lewis had told Jefferson from Fort Mandan that he would send a canoe

Though it took some time for the members of the Lewis and Clark Expedition to find the Shoshone, it is entirely possible that the natives saw them long before the white men saw the Indians, as illustrated in this Charles M. Russell painting.

and several men back with reports once the Corps reached the Falls of the Missouri. After Sacagawea's illness, he and Clark decided that they could not risk reducing the size of the expedition. They could not assume the Shoshone would be friendly, though they continued to hope they would be.

With or without Sacagawea, Lewis and Clark first had to find the Shoshone. One week after leaving the Falls, they were cheered to learn that Sacagawea had begun to recognize the land through which they were traveling. She assured them that it was the river on which her people lived and that the Three Forks of the Missouri, where Lewis and Clark hoped to find the Shoshone, were "at no great distance." Less than a week later, on July 27, the Corps reached the Three Forks, but still there was no sign of the Shoshone. Later that day Lewis described their situation bluntly:

> *We begin to feel considerable anxiety with rispect to the Snake [Shoshone] Indians. if we do not find them or some other nation who have horses I fear the successfull issue of our voyage will be very doubtfull or at all events much more difficult in it's accomplishment. we are now several hundred miles within the bosom of this wild and mountanous country, where game may rationally be expected shortly to become scarce and subsistence precarious without any information with rispect to the country not knowing how far these mountains continue, or wher to direct our course to pass them to advantage or intersept a navigable branch of the Columbia.*

Lewis remained optimistic, though. He planned to rest a few days at the Three Forks and then set out to find the Shoshone.

Into the Unknown

Chapter Six

Across the Divide

RUE TO HIS WORD, LEWIS RESTED A FEW DAYS AT the Three Forks and then, on August 1, 1805, set out to find the Shoshone. This proved a false start. Just three days later he reached another fork in the river and decided to stay in the vicinity until Clark, following behind with the men and supplies, arrived. The delay made Lewis even more anxious. By now game was growing scarce; Sergeant Ordway recorded in his journal that "we now have to live on poor venison & goat or antelopes which goes hard with us as the fatigues is hard." Lewis spoke again with Sacagawea, who assured him that the Shoshone would be either on this river or on a westward-flowing stream just beyond it, and decided to press on with a small group no matter how far it was. "It is my resolution to find them or some others, who have horses if it should

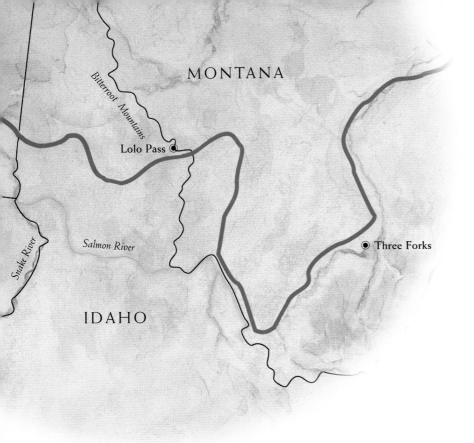

MONTANA

Bitterroot Mountains

Lolo Pass ◉

Snake River

Salmon River

◉ Three Forks

IDAHO

cause me a trip of one month," he concluded, "for without horses we shall be obliged to leave a great part of our stores, of which it appears to me that we have a stock already sufficiently small for the length of the voyage before us."

Finding the Shoshone

Lewis set out again with three men on August 9 and, to his great relief, caught sight of a Shoshone warrior two days later. Seeing a Shoshone was one thing; getting one to stop and talk was another matter. The Shoshone were not well armed, and their better-armed enemies, the Hidatsa and Blackfeet, lived to the east and northeast. The Shoshone were likely, therefore, to be extremely wary of any strangers arriving from the east. Sacagawea had done her best to prepare Lewis for this first encounter. She tried to teach him to say something appropriate in Shoshone. Lewis thought the phrase she taught him was "tab-ba-bone" and that it meant "white man." What it really was or meant no one knows. There is no Shoshone word "tab-ba-bone," and since the tribe had never before seen Europeans they

may not even have had a word for them. Some experts think that what Lewis was trying to say was simply "stranger," while others think it would have translated as something like "man who comes from where the sun rises." Whatever it was, the Shoshone did not respond. Undaunted, Lewis pulled up his shirtsleeve so that the Indian could see his whiteness (his suntanned face and hands were "quite as dark as their own"), but the Indian turned and rode off as fast as he could.

Lewis was angry and disappointed as the Shoshone rode off, writing in his journal that "with him vanished all my hopes of obtaining horses for the preasent." But at least he knew now that Shoshone were in the neighborhood. For the remainder of that day and all of the next, Lewis and his companions looked for more Indians. They found signs of them but no actual Indians. Then, on August 13, it happened again: a distant sighting, an approach saying "tab-ba-bone," and fleeing Indians. Even the Shoshone dogs ran from Lewis, foiling his plan to tie some "trinkets" around their necks in an effort to attract their masters.

Later that same day, Lewis finally got the Shoshone to talk to him. The Americans surprised a trio of women and managed to get hold of two before they could escape. Lewis repeated his one Shoshone phrase and showed them his white skin, at which point "they appeared instantly reconciled." Then he gave them some beads, awls, mirrors, and paint and asked George Drouillard, the expedition's sign language interpreter, to ask the women to call back their escaped companion, which they did. When everyone had calmed down, Lewis asked the women to take him and his men to the Shoshone camp. En route they were met by sixty mounted Shoshone warriors and Cameahwait, the chief of their band. Once the women had explained to their relations what had happened, the Shoshone welcomed the Americans with enthusiastic hugs. According to Lewis, "we wer all carressed and besmeared with their grease and paint till I was heartily tired of the national hug."

Cameahwait

Lewis and his men spent the next several days with Cameahwait's band, which had been on its way east for its annual buffalo hunt. Limited as they were to communicating by sign language, which even Lewis admitted was "imperfect," the parties did not attempt serious negotiations. Lewis did ask about the road ahead and received somewhat discouraging reports. Though the Shoshone themselves did not usu-

ally travel where Lewis and Clark planned to go, they knew Nez Perce Indians who did, and the Nez Perce had reported to the Shoshone that "the road was a very bad one." According to Cameahwait, "they [the Nez Perce] had suffered excessively with hunger on the rout...as there was no game in that part of the mountains which were broken rockey and so thickly covered with timber that they could scarcely pass." Lewis preferred to overlook the details of the route, though, and concentrate on the fact

Lewis and Clark were first-rate ethnographers. Their journals contain detailed descriptions of Indian customs. In this entry, for example, Meriwether Lewis described Shoshone pipe-smoking etiquette and sketched a Shoshone pipe.

that it could be done—"that if the Indians could pass these mountains with their women and Children, that we could also pass them." He also took heart from the number of horses in Cameahwait's camp, which Drouillard estimated at four hundred.

With extravagant promises of trade and questions about their manhood, Lewis convinced or dared Cameahwait and his warriors to travel with him back toward the Three Forks of the Missouri to meet Clark and the other Americans, who were still struggling upstream with the canoes full of baggage. What followed was worthy of Hollywood. Lewis and the Shoshone returned to the Beaverhead River, a tributary of the Missouri, and waited for Clark and the Corps to arrive. When they did, Clark, Charbonneau, and Sacagawea met Lewis and Cameahwait. Years later, Clark recalled the scene for historian Nicholas Biddle:

> *When Shabs. wife [Sacagawea] joined the party she sat down and was about to interpret when in the person of Cameahwait she discovered her brother. She jumped up, ran & embraced him, & threw her blanket over him & cried profusely. He seemed moved tho' not to the same degree that she was. After some talk between them she resumed her seat & attempted to interpret for us, but was frequently interrupted by her tears.*

It was a great stroke of luck that no doubt helped in the days that followed.

By Land or by River

After talking again with Cameahwait, Lewis and Clark decided to split the party and continue either by land or by river. Lewis still hoped to find a navigable branch of the Columbia not far ahead; he wanted half of the party to push ahead to such a branch and prepare canoes while the other half came along behind with the equipment on horses. Clark listened to the

same Shoshone reports that Lewis did and was much less optimistic; he doubted that they would find any trees large enough to make canoes or, if they were able to make canoes, that they would find any stream on which to float them safely. In spite of his doubts, though, Clark agreed to lead the advance party across the Continental Divide to the Shoshones' principal village on the Lemhi River, which flowed into the Columbia via the Salmon and Snake Rivers, and test the waters there.

As Clark and his men set out with Cameahwait and most of his band, Lewis and his men prepared to follow with the baggage. The enlisted men spent several days building packsaddles, repacking the expedition's equipment, and constructing another cache for material they would not need in the next few months. Building the cache required a bit of

stealth because Lewis did not want the Shoshone to know where it was. He had it built nearly a mile (1.6km) from camp at a spot "unperceived by the Indians," and posted a sentry while construction was in progress with instructions "to discharge his gun if he perceived any of the Indians going down in that direction which was to be the signal for the men at work on the cash to desist and seperate." Then they sank the canoes in a pond to protect them until their return, loaded their baggage on the Indians' horses, and set off for Cameahwait's village.

On the way, the Corps stopped for a brief drink at the head of the last creek before they crossed the Continental Divide. For them, this was "the extreem source of the Missouri." It had taken fifteen months and more than three thousand miles (4,827km) of travel, but the Lewis and Clark Expedition had now accomplished one of its goals. Crossing to the waters of the Columbia proved easy. Sergeant Ordway reported that after drinking from "the head Spring of the Missourie" he walked about a mile (1.6km) across a ridge and drank from "the head Spring of the Columbian River running west." Unfortunately, it was only symbolic. The crossing that mattered was still ahead, and the men learned later that day that it would not be easy. When they reached Cameahwait's village they found Private John Colter with a message from Clark and the advance party, who were scouting the route ahead: "it is not navigable, no game and very mountaineous."

Clark's message ended the debate; the Corps would have to cross the Rockies on foot, which meant they had to have horses. The next morning Lewis began haggling with the

SACAGAWEA

This statue of Sacagawea, like every other portrait of her, presents an idealized image. No picture of her from life has ever been found.

been given to her at birth or when she returned to her people with Lewis and Clark. We have no idea what she looked like. Nor do we know for sure where she went after leaving Lewis and Clark, when she died, or where she died—probably in South Dakota in 1812, though some maintain it was in Wyoming in 1884.

What we do know is that she was born among the Lemhi Shoshone in what is now Idaho or western Montana about 1788. Some twelve years later, about 1800, she was captured near Three Forks, Montana by a Hidatsa raiding party and taken back to North Dakota. There Toussaint Charbonneau bought or won her from the Hidatsa in 1804 and made her one of his two wives. Early the next year she gave birth to her first child, a boy named Jean Baptiste, and headed west with Lewis and Clark. For the next twenty months this teenage mother with an infant son traveled with Lewis and Clark. She fulfilled a number of significant roles for the Corps of Discovery. She was certainly important as an interpreter and mediator among the Shoshone and as an interpreter among other western tribes, such as the Nez Perce, holding Shoshone prisoners. She also played a limited role as a guide when the Corps moved through the area around Three Forks, and according to Clark, she provided a reassuring sign to Indians along the way that the Corps of Discovery was not a war party.

Sacagawea may not have been the indispensable girl guide of legend, but she was a valuable member of the Corps of Discovery.

She is one of the most recognizable women in American history, but we really know very little about her—not even her name. Meriwether Lewis wrote her name "Sah-ca-gar me-ah"; to John Ordway she was "Sah Cah Gah"; and modern writers have employed both Sacajawea and Sakakawea in addition to the now preferred Sacagawea. The name may have been Hidatsa, meaning "bird woman," or Shoshone, meaning "boat launcher," and if it was Shoshone may have

Shoshone to buy their horses in exchange for some of the trade goods he had brought. That worked up to a point, but the Indians were reluctant to sell the thirty horses Lewis wanted unless he gave them guns and ammunition, which he was not prepared to do. When Clark arrived he joined the process and tried to convince the Indians that the faster he and Lewis got to the coast, the better the chances that they could return in time to winter among the Shoshone. That would give the Shoshone protection and allow them to winter where the buffalo did. The Indians were not persuaded, and in the end the Americans had to trade a pistol and a rifle to get the last of the horses they needed.

Over the Bitterroot Mountains

On August 30, with their loaded horses and a Shoshone guide, the expedition set off. For nearly a week the men clawed their way north through the Bitterroot Mountains, coming down finally in the Bitterroot Valley south of what is now Missoula, Montana. Continuing north down the valley they arrived at the eastern end of the Lolo Trail—the Indian route they planned to follow west across the Bitterroots. There they rested for two days, at a site they called Travelers' Rest, before starting across the mountains on September 11. It was the roughest terrain the Americans had seen or

The rapid and turbulent waters of most of the Salmon River were a great disappointment to Lewis and Clark. They had hoped to canoe down the Salmon to the Columbia but reluctantly decided it was too dangerous to risk.

would see on their entire journey. Indeed, it is some of the most rugged wilderness in the continental United States. Food was in short supply and winter was already closing in. In every journal that has survived from the Lewis and Clark Expedition, from those of the captains to that of a private, crossing the Bitterroots stands out as the most difficult part of the seven-thousand-mile (11,300km) round trip.

The trail was never more than a footpath and at times barely that. The men often had to hack their way through "verry bad thickets" to make it wide enough for the horses and packs to get through. The trail never seemed to cross level ground; men and horses were always climbing or descending slopes "nearly as steep as the roof of a house." It was so steep at times that Ordway noted when some of the weaker horses fell backward down the hill. They also fell off the side in places where the trail was little more than a narrow ledge. In one case, Lewis reported that a horse stepped off the trail and rolled nearly one hundred yards (91.5m) down the hillside. "We all expected that the horse was killed," Lewis wrote, "but to our astonishment when the load was taken off him he arose to his feet & appeared to be but little injured."

The weather was worse than the trail. It was often cloudy or raining; the men were wet for days. And it was cold. Ordway often complained that the men's fingers "aked with the cold" and recorded several mornings on which they found that their moccasins had frozen overnight. The worst day was September 16. The men woke to find themselves covered with two inches (5cm) of wet snow, and it kept falling all day, reaching a depth of six inches (15cm). It fell off the trees as men brushed them, so they were "continually covered with Snow," and it obliterated the trail at times, leading to delays while Clark and the guide looked for the trail. It was a horrible day: "I have been [as] wet and as cold in every part as I ever was in my life," wrote Clark when it was over.

Through it all, the men were on very short rations. By then they had eaten nearly all the food they had brought from St. Louis or the Mandan villages. All they had left was portable soup and what they could find around them. The Shoshone had warned Lewis and Clark that there was little game in the Bitterroots, and they were right. Hunters went out every day but came back empty-handed more often than not. They did manage to bag some pheasants and a few meager deer. The men also collected berries when they could and found some crayfish one day. Mostly, though, they seem to have lived on portable soup and the few horses they felt were expendable.

By September 18 the situation had become critical. After two weeks of mountains, cold, and hunger, the end was nowhere in sight. John Ordway wrote that afternoon that "the Mountains continues as fer as our eyes could extend." As for their food, Lewis wrote, "a few canesters of [soup]..., a little bears oil and about 20 lbs. [9kg] of candles form our stock of provision." When that was gone they would have no choice but to eat the packhorses on which they were depending to carry their equipment. To avoid that last desperate measure, Clark and six hunters went ahead, hoping to break out of the mountains into better hunting country and send food back to the main party coming down behind them. Two days later, on September 20, Clark and his men had still found no game, but they did find the Nez Perce Indians.

Three weeks after they had set out through the mountains, Clark and his men came to a Nez Perce village on a small tributary of the Clearwater River, in what is now northern Idaho. From the villagers they were able to buy salmon and camas root—a starchy root from which the Indians made bread. They bought enough for themselves and to send back to their companions, who were "half Starved and very weak" by the time it arrived. Cheered by the food and by the knowledge that they were almost out of the mountains, Lewis and his party pressed on, and by September 22 the entire Corps of Discovery had made it to the Nez Perce village. They had crossed the Rockies. Ahead somewhere lay the Pacific.

Across the Divide

September 15, 1805 *From this mountain I could observe high ruged mountains in every direction as far as I could See. with the greatest exertion we Could only make 12 miles up this mountain and encamped on the top of the mountain near a Bank of old Snow about 3 feet deep lying on the Northern Side of the mountain and in Small banks on the top & leavel parts of the mountain, we melted the Snow to drink, and Cook our horse flesh to eat.*

William Clark

The Rockies, Lewis and Clark learned, were nothing like the Appalachian Mountains with which they were familiar. The Rockies were taller and more rugged than the Appalachians and were often covered with snow by early fall.

Across the Divide

Chapter Seven

To the Coast

WHEN THE CORPS REACHED THE NEZ Perce villages, they needed food, rest, and canoes. Clark wrote that the men were "weacke and much reduced in flesh as well as Strength." Their first priority, therefore, was food. The men gorged themselves on salmon and camas and soon paid a price. Something made them very sick. Perhaps it was the sudden change in diet or perhaps some of the fish had spoiled. Whatever it was, within a few days virtually the entire Lewis and Clark Expedition was complaining of diarrhea and indigestion, and for several days many of the men were too sick even to walk: "So unwell that they were Compelled to lie on the Side of the road for Some time."

Illness and the lingering effects of their ordeal on the Lolo Trail also left the men too weak to fashion canoes in their

PACIFIC OCEAN

WASHINGTON

Columbia River

OREGON

Snake River

PAGE 88: *Beacon Rock,*
now a Washington State
Park, still looks much as
it did when Lewis and
Clark described it in the
autumn of 1805. The core
of an ancient volcano, the
monolith rises 800 feet
(244m) above the
Columbia River. Both a
highway and a railroad
skirt the foot of Beacon
Rock today, but the cap-
tains would probably still
recognize what Clark
described as "a remark-
able high detached rock."
ABOVE: *After building a*
fleet of canoes, the expe-
dition sailed down the
Snake and Columbia
Rivers to the Pacific
Ocean from September
through December, 1805.

accustomed way. They quickly found trees that were large enough and managed to cut them down, but the men were too exhausted to hollow them out with axes, as they had planned to do. Fortunately, they were willing to adapt the Nez Perce method of burning out the logs, which spared them hours of hard labor, and by early October the Corps had five new canoes. While finishing the canoes, they also bought and packed food for the journey and questioned Nez Perce leaders about the river and the people ahead. And in the midst of these preparations for the trip downstream, the Americans also prepared for their return. Come spring, they would need their horses to recross the Lolo Trail; so they arranged with the Nez Perce to leave their animals in the Indians' care until they returned, branded each horse, and buried the packsaddles in a cache.

Down the Snake and Columbia Rivers

The final run to the coast began on October 7 and was unlike anything the expedition had yet experienced. It was the first time since leaving

the Ohio River, nearly two years earlier, that they were traveling downstream. That spared them the arduous task of rowing or pulling their boats upstream but exposed them to the very real risk of losing their boats or their lives in a sudden encounter with one of the many rapids they had to negotiate. During their first full day on the river, the Corps had to run fifteen rapids. While navigating the last of these, one of the canoes struck a rock, cracked, and began taking on water. Several of the men on board were unable to swim and found themselves clinging to a submerged canoe in the middle of the river. "Their they Stayed in this doleful Situation untill we unloaded one of the other canoes and went and released them," wrote Sergeant Ordway.

During their first three weeks on the Snake and Columbia Rivers, Lewis and Clark were constantly unloading and loading the canoes—either to portage around a rapid or waterfall or to dry supplies that had gotten wet when they ran the rapids. In spite of the delays this entailed, the Corps often made thirty to forty miles (18 to 14km) in a day. They also lost significant quantities of food and supplies, though, including some of the trade goods they planned to use as currency on their way back.

Interaction With the Natives

The trip down the Snake and Columbia Rivers was also unusual in the frequency of contact between red and white Americans. Until now, contact between Indians and the Lewis and Clark Expedition had been relatively limited except during the winter at Fort Mandan. There had been long intervals between Indian settlements on the Missouri because most of the tribes living there moved away from the river to hunt buffalo every summer, and few tribes lived in the mountains along the Lolo Trail. West of the mountains the density of the Indian population increased as a result of the abundant supplies of salmon and other fish.

PAGE 91: *Where the Snake River joined the Columbia, the expedition first encountered natives who flattened their heads as a mark of ethnic identity. "All the women have flat heads pressed to almost a point at top,"* wrote Clark: *"They press the female childrens heads between 2 boards when young—untill they form the Skul as they wish it which is generally very flat. This amongst these people is considered as a great mark of buty."*
ABOVE: *Eastern Washington's Palouse region posed a different sort of challenge to the expedition than the Rockies had, but it was just as frustrating. Because there was so little game and so little wood in this arid, prairie region, the expedition often had to rely on trade with the local Indians for food and firewood.*

Now, for the first time, the expedition came to Indian settlements every day and stopped almost daily in an Indian village or camp.

Unfortunately, members of the expedition quickly discovered a problem arising from the greater density of population along the river and the mild winters of the region: fleas. Indian villages were often alive with fleas, which saw the Americans as just another meal. "The Flees which the party got on them at the upper & great falls," wrote Clark in late October, "are very troublesom and difficult to get rid of, perticularly as the me[n] have not a Change of Clothes to put on, they Strip off their Clothes and kill the flees, dureing which time they remain neckid."

Some of the stops Lewis and Clark made at Indian settlements involved a bit of diplomacy, or ethnography, or inquiries about the river ahead, but most of them were to buy food and firewood. On either side of the river now were dry plains on which there was little to hunt beyond birds and "not a tree to be seen as far as our Eyes could extend." Most of the expedition's food in this portion of its journey came from Indian sources: salmon and dog. Most of the men came to enjoy the latter, said Clark, although he never developed a taste for it.

Many of these stops also involved disputes over property. Lewis and Clark complained constantly about the problem of Indians steal-ing the Corps' supplies. At every portage or campsite, it seemed, Indians helped themselves to whatever they could. To the whites, of course, this was theft. To the Indians, however, it was proper compensation for Indian services or an appropriate reminder to the travelers of who controlled the region around them. Fortunately, none of these incidents turned violent, though they certainly did not help Indian-white relations.

By early November, Lewis and Clark could sense the coast ahead. Once they passed the Great Rapids of the Columbia, at what is now Cascades Lock, Oregon, they entered the river's tidewater and could see the rise and fall of the tides each day. They could also tell the coast was near from the Indians' possessions and language. Every Indian tribe that Lewis and Clark met on their journey owned some European goods, but as the Americans approached the Pacific the quantity of those goods increased steadily. They began to see Indians wearing sailors' jackets or hats and carrying a variety of metal items acquired in trade with ships that visited the coast in search of sea otter pelts. They also met their first English-speaking Indian in more than a year. Ordway recorded the Corps' encounter with an Indian "[who] could talk & Speak Some words [of] English such as curseing and blackguard"—picked up, no doubt, from arguments with sailors.

Entering the Lower Columbia valley, Lewis and Clark finally left the dry plateaus of eastern and central Washington and moved into this damper coastal environment.

Lewis and Clark produced two sorts of maps as they traveled through the American West. The most detailed were those they drew of the waters they had navigated themselves, such as the map (OPPOSITE) of the Long and Short Narrows of the Columbia River near what is now The Dalles, Oregon. More valuable to historians, though, are maps such as that of the region around the junction of the Columbia and Lewis (Snake) Rivers (RIGHT). Because it was drawn on the basis of Indian information it provides a rare glimpse at the world of Native Americans in the Northwest interior before European contact.

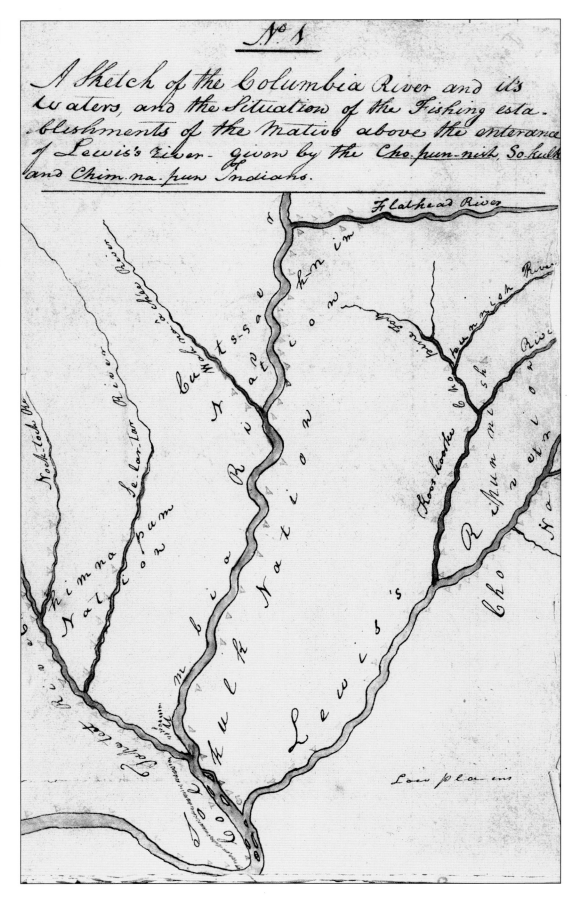

Reaching the Pacific

After eighteen months and 4,142 miles (6,664km) of travel, Lewis and Clark's arrival at the Pacific was remarkably unspectacular. There was no defining moment—no Columbus wading ashore and planting the flag. The closest one comes to that in the journals of Lewis and Clark is Clark's premature announcement, on November 7, that "we are in view of the Ocian, this great Pacific Octean which we have been So long anxious to see." In fact, they were still several miles from the ocean and were actually looking at the estuary of the Columbia River. There never was any great moment when the Lewis and Clark Expedition sailed out of the Columbia and into the waters of the Pacific. The reality was much more mundane. The canoes continued to work their way down the north shore of the Columbia until November 15, when Clark concluded, "this I could plainly See would be the extent of our journey by water, as the waves were too high at any Stage for our canoes to proceed any further down." By then, they were at the eastern end of Haley's Bay (now called Baker Bay), directly opposite the mouth of the Columbia, and Clark settled for a campsite "in full view of the Ocian."

From there, some of the men traveled by land the last few miles to visit the Pacific shore. Lewis had already taken a small party ahead a few days earlier to look for any sign of ships on the coast, and after his return, on November 18, Clark led the rest of the Corps to see the ocean. Incredible as it may seem today, nearly half the men who had crossed the continent with Lewis and Clark had no interest in going those final miles, "being well Contented with what part of the Ocean & its curiosities which Could be Seen from the vicinity of our Camp." Sergeant Ordway was one of those who did go with Clark, and his journal provides one of the few surviving accounts of the moment when he and his companions finally accomplished President Jefferson's goal of sending Americans to the Pacific:

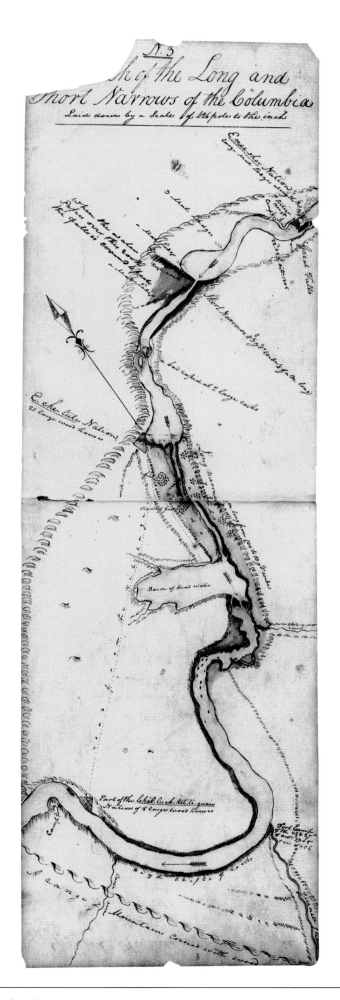

WHITE TRADERS IN THE PACIFIC NORTHWEST

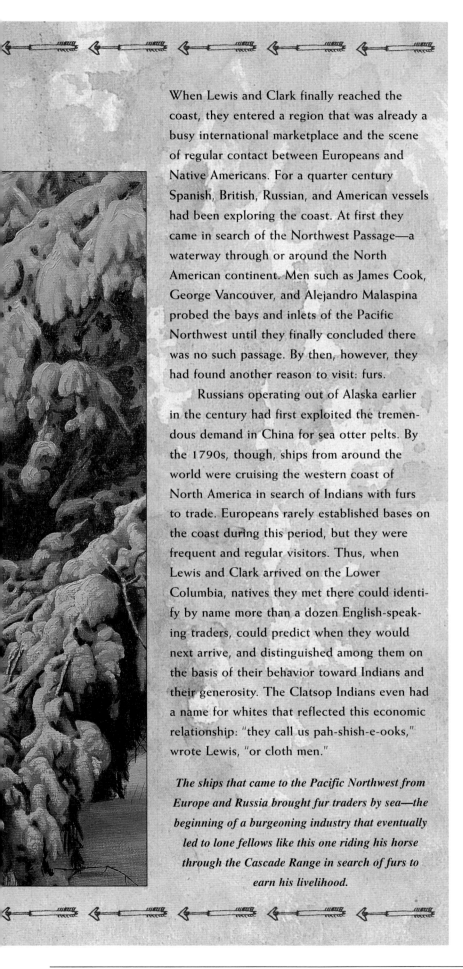

When Lewis and Clark finally reached the coast, they entered a region that was already a busy international marketplace and the scene of regular contact between Europeans and Native Americans. For a quarter century Spanish, British, Russian, and American vessels had been exploring the coast. At first they came in search of the Northwest Passage—a waterway through or around the North American continent. Men such as James Cook, George Vancouver, and Alejandro Malaspina probed the bays and inlets of the Pacific Northwest until they finally concluded there was no such passage. By then, however, they had found another reason to visit: furs.

Russians operating out of Alaska earlier in the century had first exploited the tremendous demand in China for sea otter pelts. By the 1790s, though, ships from around the world were cruising the western coast of North America in search of Indians with furs to trade. Europeans rarely established bases on the coast during this period, but they were frequent and regular visitors. Thus, when Lewis and Clark arrived on the Lower Columbia, natives they met there could identify by name more than a dozen English-speaking traders, could predict when they would next arrive, and distinguished among them on the basis of their behavior toward Indians and their generosity. The Clatsop Indians even had a name for whites that reflected this economic relationship: "they call us pah-shish-e-ooks," wrote Lewis, "or cloth men."

The ships that came to the Pacific Northwest from Europe and Russia brought fur traders by sea—the beginning of a burgeoning industry that eventually led to lone fellows like this one riding his horse through the Cascade Range in search of furs to earn his livelihood.

Capt. Clark myself and 10 more of the party set out in order to go down and see the passific ocean. we proceeded on round Hailys bay crossed two Rivers in sd bay . . . towards evening we arrived at the Cape disappointment on the Sea Shore. went over a bald hill where we had a handsom view of the ocean.

It is easy enough to understand why so many of the men showed so little interest in seeing the Pacific. Their first ten days at the mouth of the Columbia were an utterly wretched experience. It rained almost continuously. According to Clark, between November 5 and November 14 they never enjoyed more than two hours in a row without rain. The men and their baggage were "as wet as water could make them," and their leather clothing began to rot and fall apart. As if that were not enough, the men were trapped for nearly a week at a campsite that every high tide threatened to flood. As they floated down the Columbia, strong winds and tides held them up just east of Baker Bay and forced them to camp on a narrow strip of land and driftwood below the cliffs bordering the river. They remained there for six days; "our canoes at one place at the mercy of the waves, our baggage in another and our Selves and party Scattered on floating logs and Such dry Spots as can be found on the hill Sides, and Crivices of the rocks." It is hardly surprising, then, that by the time Captain Clark offered to lead an excursion to the coast most of the men wanted to head back upstream—where it was dry—and look for a place to spend the winter.

Winter Camp

Finding someplace to spend the winter was also important to Lewis and Clark, but their chief concern was not with escaping the rain. Their first priority was an adequate supply of food. They could not afford to buy food from the Indians, whose high prices would quickly

deplete the Corps' limited stock of trade goods; so they would have to rely on their own hunters. The Americans were also in desperate need of clothing, which meant that they needed deer or elk skins—preferably elk. The captains remembered how little big game they had seen as they came down the Columbia, and according to the natives they had met since reaching the river's mouth, elk were more plentiful on the south side of the river. The captains also wanted to make salt from seawater for the trip home and watch for the arrival of American or European ships, which meant staying near the coast, but these goals were secondary to food and clothing.

After discussing all this with members of the expedition, the captains asked them to vote in a meeting held on November 24. There were apparently two votes that day. First, should they cross the river and examine the south shore or head upstream immediately? Second, if the south shore did not meet their needs, where upstream should they go? Everyone got to vote—even Sacagawea and York—though Toussaint Charbonneau declined to cast his. On the second question there was no consensus, but on the first all except one member voted to examine the south shore first; so as soon as the weather permitted, the Corps crossed to the south side of the river.

Safely across the Columbia, the hunters fanned out in search of game, while Lewis looked for a place to build their second, and, they hoped, last winter camp. Clark and the others remained with the boats and baggage, and Clark used the time to prepare an American response to Alexander Mackenzie, the Canadian explorer whose journey had prompted Jefferson to dispatch the Lewis and Clark Expedition. In what was surely a conscious echo of the message Mackenzie had left in British Columbia, Clark carved on a large pine: "William Clark December 3 1805. By Land from the U. States in 1804 & 1805." The United States had reached the Pacific.

November 8, 1805 *Some rain all day at intervales, we are all wet and disagreeable, as we have been for Several days past, and our present Situation a verry disagreeable one in as much, as we have not leavel land Sufficient for an encampment and for our baggage to lie cleare of the tide, the High hills jutting in so close and steep that we cannot retreat back, and the water of the river too Salt to be used, added to this the waves are increasing to Such a hight that we cannot move from this place, in this Situation we are compelled to form our camp between the bite of the Ebb and flood tides, and raise our baggage on logs. . . . The seas roled and tossed the Canoes in such a manner this evening that Several of our party were Sea sick.*

Meriwether Lewis

The Corps of Discovery chose to make its winter camp on the Columbia River, in hopes of finding a relatively dry spot to wait out the cold weather. Unfortunately, as they discovered, the wet climate of the region allows for beautiful, lush scenery but provides no dry areas to winter in.

Chapter Eight

Waiting at Fort Clatsop

ATE IN MARCH 1806, AS THE CORPS OF Discovery prepared to leave its winter camp, William Clark reflected on the months they had spent there: "At this place we had wintered and remained from the 7th of Decr. 1805 to this day and have lived as well as we had any right to expect, and we can Say that we were never one day without 3 meals of Some kind a day either pore Elk meat or roots, not withstanding the repeeted fall of rain which has fallen almost Constantly." Clark's entry summed up perfectly Lewis and Clark's second winter on the road, and in fact displays an admirable optimism in describing what had been a thoroughly disagreeable experience. The men endured a depressing winter of rain, sickness, and bad food. Everyone survived, but no one enjoyed it.

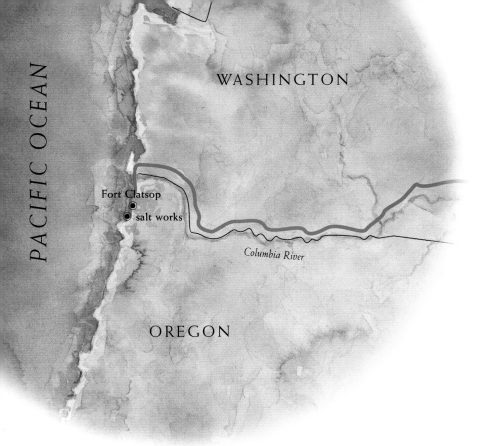

PACIFIC OCEAN

WASHINGTON

Fort Clatsop

salt works

Columbia River

OREGON

PAGE 100: *The Oregon coast is still just as beautiful as William Clark found it in 1806: "the nitches and points of high land which forms this Corse for a long ways aded to the inoumberable rocks of emence Sise out at a great distance from the Shore and against which the Seas brak with great force gives this Coast a most romantic appearance."* ABOVE: *The winter of 1805-1806 tried the patience of all the members of the Corps. Constant rain, monotonous food, and voracious fleas made everyone miserable.*

Building Fort Clatsop

It started, as Clark recalled, on December 7, when the rest of the Corps arrived at a site chosen by Captain Lewis a few days earlier. The site lay in a grove of pine and fir trees thirty feet (9m) above high tide on the bank of a small river, today named the Lewis and Clark River, that fell into Youngs Bay near the mouth of the Columbia. Three days later construction began on Fort Clatsop, named for the local Indian people. The fort was a square, some fifty feet (15m) on each side, consisting of two rows of log rooms facing one another across a central parade ground with palisades closing off the two other sides. Moving in to their new barracks on Christmas Eve and Christmas Day, the men were finally able to get dry. They could not escape the fleas, though. Just a week after moving in, Lewis complained, "we are infested with swarms of fleas already in our new habitations; the presumption is therefore strong that we shall not devest ourselves of this intolerably troublesome vermin during our residence here."

The Corps also established a small camp for salt making on the coast about fifteen miles

(24km) southwest of Fort Clatsop. From late December to late February three-man crews lived and worked at the camp turning saltwater into table salt. They filled kettles with ocean water and kept the water boiling until it evaporated, leaving a residue of salt that they could scrape out for use on their food. The camp could produce three to four quarts (2.8 to 3.8L) of salt each day, which Clark pronounced to be of "excellent" quality though not as strong as the rock salt he had seen in Kentucky. By the time the saltworks was closed, the men had filled two kegs for the trip home—more than enough to meet their needs.

Problems at the Fort

Once Fort Clatsop was completely finished, at the end of December, its occupants settled into a dull routine for the next three months. In marked contrast to the winter they spent among the Mandan, Lewis and Clark's winter on the Pacific coast was an exercise in tedium. Except for the hunters and the salt makers, few of the Americans ventured out much, and diarists frequently reported that "no occurrence worthy of relation took place today." At times it seemed that all the Corps did that winter was mark time until it could leave.

Almost the only exception to the boredom was an excursion to the coast to see a whale that was beached south of the salt camp. When word of the animal reached Fort Clatsop in early January, Clark decided to take twelve men and try to recover or buy some of the blubber. Clark did not explain how he picked his men, but one factor may have been their interest in the unusual event. That certainly motivated at least one participant: Sacagawea. She was not invited at first but eventually convinced Clark to include her. "She observed that She had traveled a long way with us to See the great waters," Clark wrote, "and that now that [a] monstrous fish was also to be Seen, She thought it verry hard that She Could not be permitted to See either (She had never yet

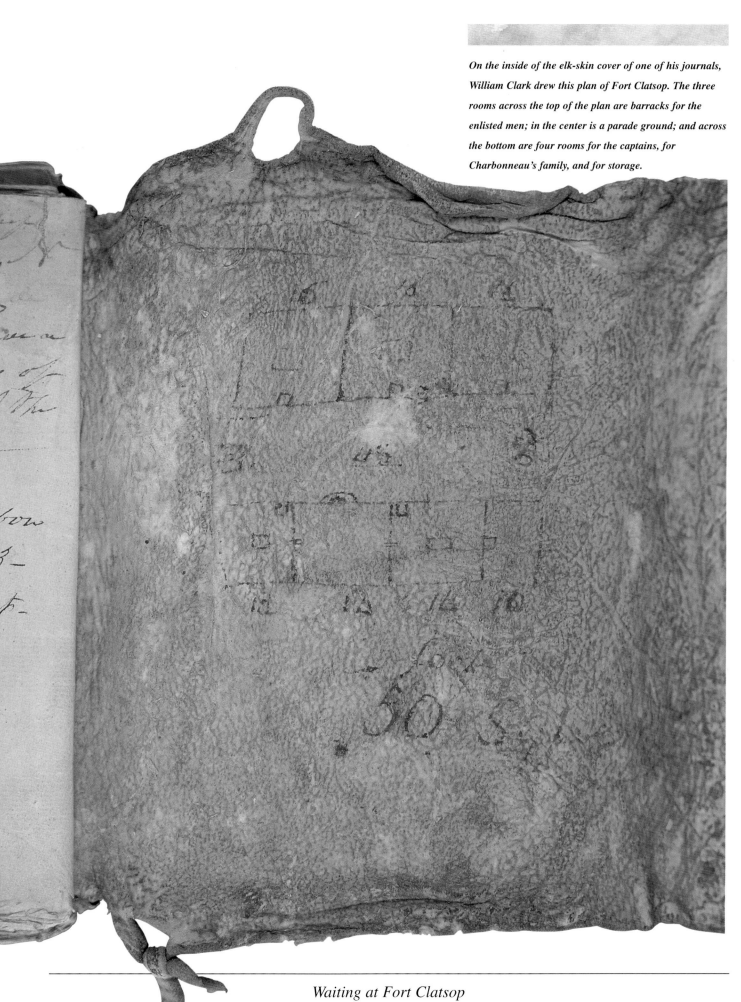

On the inside of the elk-skin cover of one of his journals, William Clark drew this plan of Fort Clatsop. The three rooms across the top of the plan are barracks for the enlisted men; in the center is a parade ground; and across the bottom are four rooms for the captains, for Charbonneau's family, and for storage.

Soon after reaching the coast, Lewis and Clark discovered that parts of the coastal Northwest are temperate rainforest. The moist environment may be ideal for ferns and moss, but it made life miserable for the Corps of Discovery. Nothing, it seemed, could keep them dry; metal rusted, food spoiled, and even their leather clothing rotted in the cool, damp climate.

tried to smoke it. Day after day the men ate boiled elk, some of it "So much spoiled that we eate it thro' mear necessity." They were soon so tired of their low-fat diet that a bit of elk with "the appearance of a little fat on it" was "liveing in high Stile."

The main problem that winter was homesickness; members of the Lewis and Clark Expedition were ready to be home. They had been traveling for more than two years. They had certainly enjoyed the trip, and their journals suggest no hint of regret that they had chosen to make it, but they were ready for it to end. Lewis and Clark had hoped to be east of the Rockies, maybe even among the Mandan again, during the winter of 1805–1806; instead they were still on the Pacific coast.

Furthermore, once they reached the coast they had accomplished their major goal. Hardship had been much easier to endure when there was still something ahead that made it worthwhile. Now, having fulfilled the President's orders, the only worthwhile objective in sight was home, and every day they spent at Fort Clatsop delayed their return.

The captains planned to leave Fort Clatsop on April 1, 1806, and their journals that winter show how eagerly they awaited that date. On New Year's Day, 1806, Lewis wrote, "Our repast of this day tho' better than that of Christmass, consisted principally in the anticipation of the 1st day of January 1807, when in the bosom of our friends we hope to participate in the mirth and hilarity of the day." A month later he noted that the only thing worth reporting that day was "that one month of the time which binds us to Fort Clatsop and which seperates us from our friends has now elapsed." And in early March he wrote, "We are counting the days which seperate us from the 1st of April and which bind us to fort Clatsop."

been to the Ocian)." The whale was only a brief distraction. The party soon returned to Fort Clatsop and resumed its mundane routine.

Weather was one of the problems. Though Lewis and Clark were pleasantly surprised by how warm the winter was, they were disgusted by the damp climate of the Pacific Northwest. It seemed to rain incessantly, often accompanied by strong winds, and even when rain was not falling it was impossible to stay dry in the high humidity. Another problem was illness. One man after another came down with various complaints that winter, and at one point an exasperated Clark wrote, "We have not had as many Sick at one time Since we left the Settlements of the Illinois." The men's monotonous diet further reduced morale. The Corps' hunters always managed to find enough elk to keep the men fed, but the meat was very lean, there was little to go with it, and in the warm climate it quickly spoiled—even when they

Indian Relations

Nowhere was the dullness of winter at Fort Clatsop more evident than in relations between

left which the string pass to fasten the round pieces which pass crosswise the Canoe to strengthen & left her. This form of a canoe we did not meet with untile we reached tide water or below the great Rapids. from thence down it is common to all the nations but more particularly the Kil a mox and others of the Coast. these are the largest canoes, I measured one at the Kelamox villag SSW of us which was   feet long .   feet wide and   feet deep, and they are most commonly about that sitze. B is the bow, and

Among the Indians around Fort Clatsop, Lewis and Clark encountered a culture unlike any they had ever met before. Natives of this region belonged to the Chinookan people and shared a number of cultural traits with other natives of the coastal Northwest. Like many other coastal Indians, Chinookans lived in a very hierarchical society in which status was linked to personal wealth and to public displays of that wealth. At the top were hereditary chiefs and their familes; at the bottom were hereditary slaves; and in the middle were upper and lower classes of common people. For nobles and commoners the ownership of slaves was an important sign of status. House size was another sign. Often 25 by 50 feet (7.6 to 15.3m), Chinookan houses were built with a

Canoes such as this one, drawn by Meriwether Lewis in 1806, were typical among tribes of the Pacific Northwest. With their carved stern and bowposts, they were beautiful works of art as well as marvelous boats.

frame of cedar posts supporting a horizontal ridge pole in the center and horizontal eaves poles on either side. The roof and sides were covered with cedar planks, and the short sides were often painted to resemble a face, with an open mouth forming the doorway.

Chinookans also made hats in a style common to the coastal Northwest and greatly admired by Lewis and Clark. Made of grass and cedar bark, these cone-shaped hats were "nearly waterproof," according to Meriwether Lewis, which made them very desirable in the damp winter at Fort Clatsop. The captains each had one custom-made for themselves and bought more for the men of the expedition.

Most of the men of the expedition rarely went to the coast, but Lewis and Clark established a small camp for salt making near the ocean, southwest of their main camp. There the men harvested salt by boiling sea water.

members of the Lewis and Clark Expedition and the local Indian population. At Fort Mandan, Indians and whites found one another exotic and interesting, and the two shared a mutually beneficial activity in the corn-for-axes trade that was carried on by the expedition's blacksmith. The result had been almost daily contact between whites and Indians, which both groups found enjoyable and profitable. That was not the case at Fort Clatsop. There, Indian visits were rare and white visits to Indian settlements even rarer because neither side had much reason to visit the other.

Fort Clatsop certainly had little to offer from the Indians' perspective. By the time Lewis and Clark arrived, British and American ships had already been trading with natives of

the Pacific Northwest for a decade. Neither whites nor their technology held much fascination to the Indians anymore. They might have been more interested in the expedition if it had been well equipped with trade goods, but it was no longer. Lewis commented in his journal that winter that "two handkerchiefs would now contain all the small articles of merchandize which we possess."

For their part, Lewis and Clark did want to trade with the Indians around them, though they infrequently visited the Indian settlements because they disliked many of the local natives. The captains wanted to buy dogs and wapato roots, an edible root the natives used for food, to supplement their diet, and they especially wanted to buy an Indian canoe or two for the

This modern restoration of Fort Clatsop stands on or near the site of the original. It offers visitors an opportunity to see what life was like here for the men of the Lewis and Clark Expedition, but it does require some imagination. The new barracks lack the fleas, the smoke, and the smell of unwashed bodies with which the men lived during the three months they spent here.

Waiting at Fort Clatsop

voyage back up the Columbia. But the local Clatsop and Chinook peoples were discriminating consumers and drove hard bargains: "they are great higlers in trade and if they Conceive you anxious to purchase will be a whole day bargaining for a hand full of roots." Lewis and Clark had little the Indians wanted and could rarely afford their prices, so there was little trade between them. And apart from business, Lewis and Clark had little interest in their neighbors that winter. They considered the local tribes immoral, thievish, and physically repulsive. "I think the most wretched sight I have ever beheld is these dirty naked wenches," Lewis wrote. He had little interest in socializing with them the way he had with the Mandan.

Time Well Spent

The winter spent at Fort Clatsop was not totally wasted, though. It was productive, even if it was dull. Lewis wrote voluminous journal entries describing the plants, animals, and peoples he had encountered west of the Rockies. Clark used the time to prepare a map of the expedition's route since Fort Mandan supplemented by reports from Indian informants. It was by far the most complete map of the North American interior yet produced. Using this map, Clark was also able to plan the return trip and shorten it by hundreds of miles. He knew now that the Missouri River turned south at the Great Falls and that the Corps, having followed the river, had then gone north again before turning west to pass through the mountains. On the return trip, Clark planned to travel due east through the mountains and strike the Missouri closer to the Falls, cutting some six hundred miles (965km) off the journey. As for the men of the expedition, they spent the winter rebuilding their wardrobes, which had been decimated by heavy use and by the weather. By the time they left Fort Clatsop, they had new shirts and pants and 358 pairs of elk-skin moccasins.

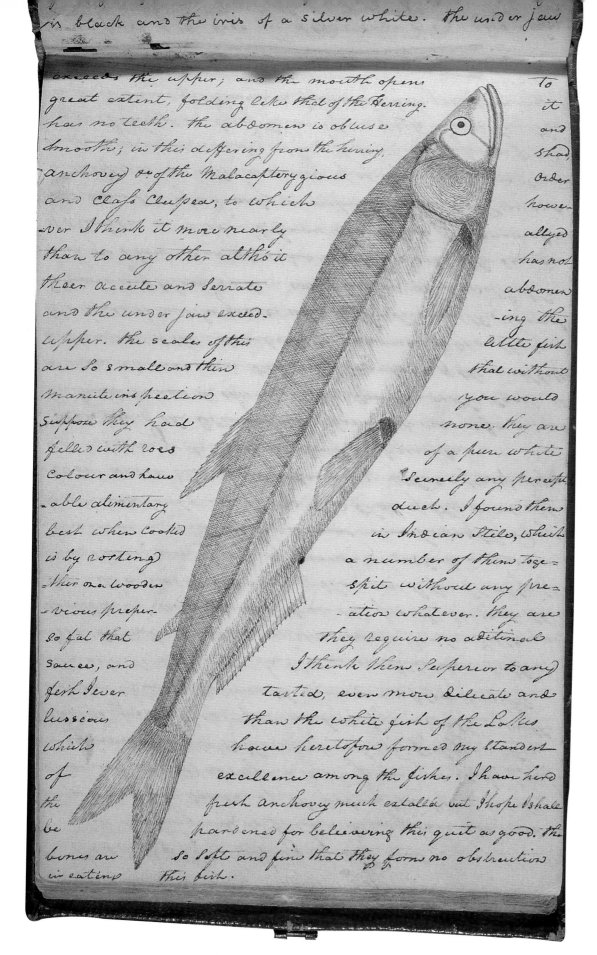

is black and the iris of a silver white. the under jaw exceeds the upper; and the mouth opens to great extent, folding like that of the Herring. has no teeth. the abdomen is obtuse and smooth; in this differing from the herring, anchovey &c. of the Malacapterygious and Class Clupea, to which however I think it more nearly than to any other altho' it their acute and Serrate and the under jaw exceed. upper. the scales of this are So small and thin that without manute inspection you would Suppose they had none. they are felled with roes of a pure white colour and have scarcely any perceptable alimentary duck. I found them best when cooked in Indian Stile, which is by roasting a number of them toge-ther on a wooden spit without any pre--vious prepa---ation whatever. they are So fat that they require no aditional Sauce, and I think them Superior to any fish I ever tasted, even more delicate and lussious than the white fish of the Lakes which have heretofore formed my standerd of excellence among the fishes. I have herd the fresh anchovey much extolled but I hope I shall be pardoned for believing this quit as good. the bones are So Soft and fine that they form no obstruction in eating this fish.

During the winter he spent at Fort Clatsop, Meriwether Lewis had a chance to demonstrate fully his skills as a naturalist and an artist. His journals for the period are filled with sketches of plants and animals, many of which no scientist had ever seen before. On the left is Lewis' drawing of a eulachon—which ran like salmon up the Columbia and Lewis thought "superior to any fish I ever tasted"; on the opposite page are his renderings of the dull Oregon grape (an evergreen shrub) leaf, a Christmas fern, and a Sitka spruce cone.

March 17, 1806 *Drewyer returned late this evening from the Cathlahmahs with our canoe which Sergt. Pryor had left some days since, and also a canoe which he had purchased from those people. for this canoe he gave my uniform laced coat and nearly half a carrot of tobacco. it seems that nothing excep[t] this coat would induce them to dispose of a canoe which in their mode of traffic is an article of the greatest val[u]e except a wife, with whom it is equal, and is generally given in exchange to the father for his daughter. I think the U'States are indebted to me another Uniform coat for that of which I have disposed on this occasion was but little woarn.*

Meriwether Lewis

Leaving Fort Clatsop

By mid-March Lewis and Clark were desperate to leave Fort Clatsop, but they knew it would be foolish to go very far inland any earlier than April 1 because of the weather. Indians had told them that east of the coastal mountains, on the Columbia Plateau, snow was knee-deep during the winter, and coming downstream in the fall the Americans had seen for themselves how scarce firewood was on the plateau. Thus, they had planned to stay on the coast until April 1, when they thought it would be warm enough to venture inland safely. As winter wore on, though, Lewis and Clark began to worry that if it started to rain heavily in late March they would have to delay their departure beyond April 1. That prospect clearly upset them. Rather than spend a single extra day at Fort Clatsop, they decided to leave early, even if that meant leaving the mild coastal climate before winter had really loosened its grip on the Columbia Plateau.

The captains also showed their impatience to leave Fort Clatsop in their calculated decision to steal an Indian canoe. Lewis and Clark had often admired the native boats and their ability to withstand much worse wind and water conditions than their own small canoes could. For the return trip up the Columbia they badly wanted some of these native canoes, but they were much too expensive for the Corps to purchase. Lewis did finally manage to buy one canoe, which cost him his best uniform jacket, but he wanted another canoe, and he wanted it badly enough to rationalize stealing one from the Clatsop. According to Lewis and Clark, the Clatsop had taken six elk killed by expedition hunters earlier that winter without paying for them, so the Americans decided to take a canoe "in lue of the six Elk."

The captains knew that six elk would never pay for a Clatsop canoe, "which in their mode of traffic is an article of the greatest value except a wife." They used the elk to justify to themselves a unilateral action they knew to be wrong and never told the Clatsop what they

---

Waiting at Fort Clatsop

were doing or why. Nor did they ever describe the actual theft; after deciding to steal a canoe they never mentioned it again. Sergeant Ordway was more candid. He wrote in his journal the next day: "4 men went over to the prarie near the coast to take a canoe which belongd to the Clatsop Indians, as we were in want of it . . . [They] took the canoe near the fort and concealed it, as the chief of the Clatsops is now here." Such a premeditated theft was not only unprecedented on Lewis and Clark's part, it was also stupid. The expedition was outnumbered by the Indians; the men were far from home; and they might still need Indian goodwill to survive. More than anything, this foolish episode shows how completely desperate the Americans were to get away from Fort Clatsop.

By March 17, 1806, Lewis and Clark had decided to leave as soon as the weather would permit. The next day they stole the Clatsop canoe they needed, and five days later, on March 23, the wind and rain finally let up. "At 1 P.M.," wrote Lewis, "we bid a final adieu to Fort Clatsop." Lewis and Clark were on their way home.

Late in March the Corps of Discovery turned its back on the Pacific and headed back up the Columbia—toward the Rockies, the Missouri River, and home.

Chapter Nine

Starting for Home

OR MEMBERS OF THE LEWIS AND CLARK Expedition, the journey home from Fort Clatsop was unlike anything they had experienced since leaving St. Louis. For the first time in two years, they were traveling through a land they already knew. Their journals of the return trip contain numerous references to familiar landmarks and campsites and to reunions with individual Indians they knew and trusted from earlier encounters. For all the uncertainty and danger that still lay ahead, members of the expedition demonstrated a familiarity with the challenges they met and a confidence in themselves based on experience rather than bravado. In a few instances, this may have made them a bit overconfident, but in general it served them well. It gave them the will to be bold when it was necessary and the

WASHINGTON

Travelers' Rest ◉
Lolo Pass ◉

◉ Fort Clatsop
◉ salt works

Columbia River

Snake River

Salmon River

IDAHO

OREGON

wisdom to be cautious when that was more appropriate.

PAGE 112: *Where it passes through the Cascade Mountains the Columbia River's gorge is so much deeper than the surrounding country that many of its tributaries drop over falls such as Multnomah Falls, in Oregon's Mt. Hood National Forest.*
ABOVE: *Lewis and Clark headed back up the Columbia River in March, 1806, but they still had to wait for snow to melt before recrossing the Rockies in July.* OPPOSITE: *Rushing streams such as this one swelled with snow runoff as the season wore on, making the climate even wetter.*

Preparing to Recross the Rockies

Caution was certainly called for on the first leg of the return, from Fort Clatsop to the start of the Lolo Trail. Memories of the Lolo Trail haunted Lewis and Clark as they ascended the Columbia that spring and drove them to look for more food and more horses wherever they could. "Not any of us have yet forgotten our sufferings in those mountains in September last," Lewis wrote, "and I think it probable we never shall." At every stop they made, the Americans tried to buy salmon, dogs, wapato, or camas roots, and once they were among tribes with horses again they tried to buy those too, both for transportation and for food.

Unfortunately, they had little with which to pay for such purchases, so they had to be creative. As Lewis explained it, "Having exhausted all our merchandize we are obliged to have recourse to every subterfuge in order to prepare in the most ample manner in our power

to meet that wretched portion of our journey, the Rocky Mountain." Their most frequent subterfuge was medicine. Clark had treated a few Indians the preceding fall when he passed through on his way to the coast. They had praised him to others, and on his return people flocked to him for medical treatment. Now he refused to provide it except in trade for food or horses, even though he doubted that he was really helping many of his patients. He justified his actions as needful and innocent: "in our present Situation I think it pardonable to continue this deception for they will not give us any provisions without Compensation in merchendize, and...we take Care to give them no article which Can possibly injure them." In another case Clark used the mysterious technology he possessed to force a sale. When a native family he was visiting refused to sell any wapato for the items he offered in trade, he threw a piece of fuse in their fire, "which changed the Colour of the fire," and used a magnet to make the needle of his compass spin wildly. This so frightened the Indians that they offered Clark several bundles of wapato to take out the "bad fire." He took the roots but paid what he thought they were worth.

Lewis and Clark were also very interested in trading for horses so that the Corps could leave its boats behind. They knew it would be faster and easier to travel by land if they could find enough horses to carry their baggage. As they moved farther inland, staying on the river would mean more and more time spent hauling their canoes and equipment around or through the rapids and waterfalls of the Columbia and its tributaries. It would also mean traveling extra miles around the bends of the rivers. Local Indians were happy to show them the trails by which they might cross the region, but it took time to find and buy enough horses. A month after leaving Fort Clatsop, and about halfway between the Fort and the junction of the Snake and Columbia Rivers, they finally had enough horses to carry their equipment and Private William Bratton, who was too ill to walk. After they sold their canoes, they set off

Starting for Home

our fire in great numbers insomuch that we scarcely cook of keep ourselves warm. at all these lodges of the Chopunnish I observe an appendage of a small lodge with one fire which seems to be the retreat of their women in a certain situation. the men are not permitted to approach this lodge within a certain distance and if they have any thing to convey to the occupents of this little hospital they stand at the distance of 50 or 60 paces and throw it toward them as far as they can and retire.

Monday May 5th 1806.
Collected our horses and set out at 7. A.M. at 4½ miles we arrived at the entrance of the Kooskooske, it the N. Eastern side of which we continued our march 12 Ms. to a large lodge of 10 families having proped two other large mat lodges the one at 5 and the other at 8 Ms. from the mouth of the Kooskooske but not being able to obtain any provision at either of those lodges continued our march to the third where we arrived at 1. P.M. & with much difficulty obtained 2 dogs, and a small quantity of bread and dryed roots. at the second lodge we proped an indian man gave Capt. C. a very eligant grey mare for which he requested a phial of eye-water which was accordingly given him. while we were encamped last fall at the entrance of the Chopunnish river Capt. C. gave an indian man some volitile linniment to rub his knee and thye for a pain of which he complained, the fellow soon after recovered and has never ceased to extol the virtues of our medecines and the skill of my friend Capt. C. as a phisician. this occurrence added to the benefit which many of them experienced from the eyewater we gave them about the same time has given them an exalted opinion of our medicine. my friend Capt. C. is their favorite phisician and has already received many applications. in our present situation I think it proper and reasonable to continue this deseption for they will not give us any provision without compensation in merchandize and our stock is now reduced to

As they traveled up the Columbia, Lewis and Clark offered medical treatment to the local Indians in exchange for horses and badly needed supplies of food. In this journal entry from May 5, 1806, Meriwether Lewis describes the medical care provided by William Clark—the natives' "favorite phisician."

As the Corps of Discovery made its way home from Fort Clatsop, Indians frequently approached Captain Clark for medical care. The natives' most common complaint was sore eyes and partial blindness. Clark thought the problems might be the results of sunlight reflected into the eyes of people who spent their lives near or on the Columbia River, though modern scholars think it was probably a form of conjunctivitis. In an effort to treat it, Clark prepared an eyewash made of zinc sulphate and lead acetate mixed in water. This probably did nothing to cure the patients, but, wrote Clark, "I believe will render them more esential Sirvece than any other article in the Medical way which we had it in our power to bestow on them."

Medical help passed both ways, though. William Bratton, a private in the Corps of Discovery, had begun to suffer "a violent pain in the small of his back" soon after the Corps settled in for the winter at Fort Clatsop. By the time the expedition started for home, Bratton was unable to work or to walk, and Clark could do little for him. Finally, another member of the Corps suggested what seems to have been an Indian sweat lodge. The men dug a large hole in which they built a fire. Once the ground was hot the fire was removed. Bratton then sat in the hole, naked, under a tent made of blankets and sprinkled water on the earth to create "as much steam or vapor as he could possibly bear." After twenty minutes, the patient was taken out, plunged twice into cold water, and returned to the sweat lodge. After a second dose of steam he was covered in blankets and "suffered to cool gradually." The next day, wrote Lewis, Bratton was "nearly free from pain," and within two weeks he had recovered completely.

on foot. This marked the beginning of a frequent pattern on the expedition's return trip: a departure from their outbound route, based on information provided by Indians, that shortened the trip by days or even weeks.

They had reason to hurry at this stage. The Nez Perce Indians with whom Lewis and Clark had left the horses they brought over the Lolo Trail had told the Americans that they planned to head east themselves as soon as the mountain passes were clear of snow. Lewis and Clark assumed the snow would be gone by the beginning of May. If the Corps did not reach the Nez Perce villages before the tribe started east, they might never find their horses, and without their horses it might be impossible to recross the Rockies. With this in mind they pushed ahead as fast as they could.

Back With the Nez Perce

One week into May they found the Nez Perce. More important, they found the horses left in their care and the packsaddles cached nearby. With the horses they had just bought, they now had more than sixty animals—enough to carry them and their baggage. Unfortunately, they also learned from the Nez Perce that the mountain snow was still so deep that the Indians thought it would be the first of June, or even later, before the Corps could safely hazard the Lolo Trail. This was, the captains both wrote, "unwelcom inteligence to men confined to a diet of horsebeef and roots, and who are as anxious as we are to return to the fat plains of the Missouri and thence to our native homes." It was clearly unwelcome news to Lewis and Clark as well. They knew that they had to accept it and wait a little longer, but their journals reveal the struggle this involved. Ten days after their arrival among the Nez Perce, Lewis forced himself to temper his excitement at the rising level of the Clearwater River, which he took to be a sign that the mountain snows were melting. "I am pleased at finding the river rise

so rapidly," he wrote; "it now doubt is attribute-able to the me[l]ting snows of the mountains; that icy barier which seperates me from my friends and Country, from all which makes life esteemable—patience, patience."

The Corps used its forced leisure to conduct diplomacy and make further preparations for crossing the mountains. The first order of business was a council with the Nez Perce chiefs. Hurrying west in the fall, Lewis and Clark had not had time for any lengthy discussions; now they had time, Lewis wrote, "to enter more minutely into the views of our government with rispect to the inhabitants of this western part of the continent." And it did take time, as every word had to pass through five different languages. Lewis and Clark's English went through translator François Labiche's French, Charbonneau's Hidatsa, and Sacagawea's Shoshone before a Shoshone boy living among the Nez Perce translated it one last time. Then the Nez Perce response had to go back along the same tedious chain of interpreters. It was slow, and a great deal was lost in the translations, but Lewis pronounced everyone "highly pleased" with the results.

The captains were also pleased with the results of their latest effort to collect food. They divided the Corps' remaining trade goods among the individual members and put every man into business for himself. Each received an awl, a knitting needle, half an ounce (14g) of paint, two needles, a few skeins of thread, and a yard (91.5cm) of ribbon to trade for whatever food he could find. Lewis admitted it was "a slender stock indeed with which to lay in a store of provision," but the results were surprisingly good. By early June, Clark was able to report, "our whole party have a Sufficient Store of bread and roots for our Voyage. a Circumstance not unpleasing."

In the end, Lewis and Clark spent nearly a month waiting for the snow to melt. Not until June 10 did they move their camp to Weippe Prairie, at the western end of the Lolo Trail, to make final preparations for the mountain crossing. Some of the Nez Perce thought they

should wait even longer, and the captains themselves still had concerns. They were worried about finding enough food for their horses along the higher parts of the trail and were uncomfortable with their failure to secure a guide—"even now I Shudder with the expectation," wrote Clark—but further delay was unthinkable. "We have not now any time to delay if the calculation is to reach the United States this season," Lewis concluded. "This I am detirmined to accomplish if within the compass of human power." On June 15, Lewis and Clark started up the Lolo Trail.

Up the Lolo Trail

The Nez Perce were right; it was too soon. Snow was still eight to ten feet (2.5 to 3m) deep in places, and though strong enough to support the horses it obliterated the trail. After two days the Corps admitted defeat. Lewis explained in his journal that it was his duty to order a return to Weippe Prairie: "If we proceeded and should get bewildered in these mountains the certainty was that we should

loose all our horses and consequently our baggage instruments perhaps our papers and thus eminently wrisk the loss of the discoveries which we had already made if we should be so fortunate as to escape with life." Jefferson had told Lewis to protect at all costs the information he gained. Hard as it must have been, he and Clark obeyed the President's orders and turned around.

The setback was only temporary. While most of the party returned to Weippe Prairie, two men were sent to the Nez Perce in a final effort to hire an Indian guide. They were authorized to offer as much as three guns in payment, an extraordinary price. It took only two. On June 23 two Nez Perce guides met Lewis and Clark at Weippe Prairie, where members of the Corps had been hunting without much success (including a futile effort to shoot trout). The next day they started again up the Lolo Trail.

The snow was still seven feet (2m) deep in many places, but somehow the guides were able to find their way. They also knew from experience where the snow tended to melt first, which meant that the Corps could be sure of stopping each night at a clearing with grass to feed its horses. Lewis and Clark were astonished and relieved by their guides' ability. Standing atop a ridge one afternoon, Lewis wrote, "From this place we had an extensive view of these stupendous mountains principally covered with snow like that on which we stood; we were entirely surrounded by those mountains from which to one unacquainted with them it would have seemed impossible ever to have escaped...these fellows are most admireable pilots." Six days after they started, on June 30, the guides brought Lewis and Clark to Travelers' Rest and the eastern end of the Lolo Trail. Though they had not yet crossed the Continental Divide and reentered the watershed of the Missouri, the worst of the Rockies was behind them.

Starting for Home

Chapter Ten

Separations and Reunions

THE WORST WAS BEHIND THEM NOW. AFTER crossing the Rockies, Lewis and Clark were still more than two thousand miles (3,200km) from St. Louis, but they had horses to ride as far as the Missouri River and then it was all downstream. They had yet to deal with the Falls of the Missouri, but they had passed these before and had much less baggage to carry this time. And while the men were out of nearly everything, they still had plenty of gunpowder and shot and would soon be back among the buffalo and deer of the Great Plains.

Splitting Up the Corps

The captains planned to spend a few days recuperating at Travelers' Rest before setting off on the boldest—some say

Lewis' fight with the Blackfeet

Milk River

Corps' reunion

Marias River

Travelers' Rest

MONTANA

Yellowstone River

Missouri River

Pompy's Tower

Tongue River

Powder River

WYOMING

IDAHO

most foolish—portion of their coast-to-coast journey. To gather as much information as they could without delaying their return, Lewis and Clark had decided to divide the Corps into several smaller expeditions. Clark and most of the men would travel back to the canoes they had left earlier on the headwaters of the Missouri. From there, Sergeant Ordway and nine men would float down the Missouri, while Clark and ten others crossed to the Yellowstone River. On reaching the Yellowstone, Clark was to send Sergeant Nathaniel Pryor with two privates and most of the Corps' horses overland to the Mandan villages and on to the Assiniboine River, in modern Manitoba, with a letter to Hugh Heney, a British fur trader with links to the Teton Sioux, asking his help in convincing the Sioux to send a delegation to Washington. Clark and the rest of his party would then build a canoe and sail down the Yellowstone to its junction with the Missouri. Lewis, in the meantime, would take nine men with him to the Falls of the Missouri, leave three men at the Falls to prepare wheels and axles for a portage, and take the others with him to explore Marias River. The trio left at the Falls would wait for Ordway to arrive with the canoes, portage

around the Falls, and continue down the Missouri, picking up Lewis at the mouth of Marias River and Clark at the mouth of the Yellowstone.

Once they separated, of course, Lewis and Clark would have no way of communicating with each other. A successful reunion would depend on their skill and on the geographical knowledge they had acquired through their travels and their conversations with Native Americans. Dividing the Corps also meant reducing its military strength, which the captains had often maintained was all that protected them from Indian "insults." It was an enormous gamble, and they must have known the risk they were taking when they separated on July 3. Yet all that either man wrote of their parting was a brief comment in Lewis' journal: "I took leave of my worthy friend and companion Capt. Clark and the party that accompanied him. I could not avoid feeling much concern on this occasion although I hoped this separation was only momentary."

Until the Corps reassembled at full strength, its members would be dangerously exposed to Indian raiders attracted by the Americans' horses and equipment. Such a raid could easily escalate into serious violence that threatened the expedition's goal of establishing good relations with natives of the Missouri Valley—if not the Americans' very survival. That danger was certainly on the captains' minds as they parted at Travelers' Rest, but they believed the potential benefits to be gained from the separation outweighed the risk.

Back to the Missouri

Lewis left Travelers' Rest with nine men and seventeen horses. He and his party rode north down the Bitterroot Valley to the junction of the Bitterroot and Blackfoot Rivers, just west of modern Missoula, Montana. There they turned east and followed an Indian road up the Blackfoot to the Continental Divide—an "easy ascent," Lewis noted. After crossing the divide

Indians and Guns

The skirmish between Meriwether Lewis and the Piegan Blackfeet had little to do with hostility between Indians and whites. Rather, it was the tragic result of an intertribal arms race that shows how white men's technology affected native life long before white men themselves arrived on the northern Plains.

As British and French fur traders expanded across Canada during the 1700s, guns were one of the items they offered in trade and the item most eagerly sought by their Indian trading partners. Even a few guns gave tribes that had them a tremendous advantage over those that did not in the competition for hunting grounds or in the raids on one another that were endemic to Native American life . As a result, tribes closer to the trading posts, such as the Cree, Assiniboines, and Sioux, did their best to prevent more distant tribes from gaining direct access to whites and their guns. This is why the Nez Perce and Shoshone had tried so hard to get guns in exchange for their food or horses and one of the reasons they were so willing to help Lewis and Clark. Neither the Nez Perce nor the Shoshone had guns or ready access to Canadian traders, and they saw the Americans as an immediate and future source of guns.

This native competition for guns is also what led to Meriwether Lewis's clash with the Piegan Blackfeet. When Lewis arrived on the Marias River, the Blackfeet were trying to stop Assiniboine expansion into their traditional homeland. Beaver were growing scarce in Assiniboine territory; so the tribe was looking for new sources to tap and using its superior firepower to encroach on Blackfeet territory. The Piegans Lewis met had nothing against the Americans and apparently did not intend to hurt them. They simply wanted their rifles. Unfortunately, Lewis' men were equally determined not to surrender them. The result was a clash that killed at least one Piegan and, some believe, triggered years of Blackfeet anger toward white Americans.

This print from Patrick Gass' journal depicts the skirmish between Meriwether Lewis' party and a band of Piegan Blackfeet. The artist has shown four men with Lewis, though there were actually just three.

Indians also became a major concern again once Lewis reached the Missouri. Ten of his seventeen horses disappeared one night, presumably stolen by Indians. This forced Lewis to reduce by half the number of men he could take to explore Marias River, which was particularly worrisome because Marias River lay in a region frequented by tribes of the Blackfeet confederation. The Corps had not yet met any Blackfeet, but the natives' reputation preceded them: "they are a vicious lawless and reather an abandoned set of wretches," Lewis wrote. Now he had only enough horses for three men to accompany him, which would leave him even more vulnerable to the Blackfeet. "I have no doubt," he wrote, "but they would steel our horses if they have it in their power and finding us weak should they happen to be numerous wil most probably attempt to rob us of our arms and baggage; at all events I am determined to take every possible precaution to avoid them if possible."

they continued north to the Sun River and followed the Sun east to its junction with the Missouri, just above the Falls of the Missouri. On reaching the Falls, they returned to the Corps' upper portage camp, recovered the equipment they had buried there twelve months earlier, and began to prepare for the arrival of Sergeant Ordway and the canoes.

It was a welcome relief to be back on the Missouri. After nearly a year of living on lean elk, horse, dog, fish, camas, and wapato, the men could feast on buffalo again. When Lewis reached the portage camp on July 12, he wrote, "I sincerely belief that there were not less than 10 thousand buffaloe within a circle of 2 miles [3.2km] around that place." By noon his hunters had killed eleven buffalo, and by 3 P.M. the party had "a large quantity of fine beef." Unfortunately, returning to the Missouri also meant renewed conflict with grizzly bears. Three days after reaching the river, Corps member Hugh McNeal was nearly killed by a grizzly he surprised in some thick brush. When the bear reared to defend itself, McNeal's horse took fright and threw him almost under the beast. All McNeal had time to do was club the bear with his rifle, which broke in half from the blow, and scramble up a willow tree while the grizzly "fell to the ground and began to scratch his head with his feet." The bear kept McNeal treed for three hours before it gave up and left.

To Marias River

Leaving six men at the Falls of the Missouri to await the canoes and continue downstream with Sergeant Ordway, Lewis and three others set out to explore Marias River. For several days the quartet rode north and west without incident, finding and following Marias River and its northern fork in an effort to discover how far north they extended. Once the stream began turning southwest, just east of what is now Glacier National Park, Lewis decided he had gone far enough and prepared to return to the Missouri. At that point his luck ran out. On July 26 he encountered a small party of Piegan Blackfeet. "This was a very unpleasant sight," Lewis wrote. "However I resolved to make the best of our situation and to approach them in a friendly manner." The meeting actually went quite well, and the two parties agreed to camp together that night. Lewis was still cautious, though; he took the first watch himself and warned his relief to watch the Piegan carefully.

saddled. this was a very unpleasent sight, however I resolved to make the best of our situation and to approach them in a friendly manner. I directed J. Fields to display the flag which I had brought for that purpose and advanced slowly towards them, about this time they discovered us and appeared to run about in in a very confused manner as if much allarmed, their attention had been previously so fixed on Drewyer that they did not discover us untill we had began to advance upon them, some of them decended the hill on which they were and drove their horses within shot of it's summit and again returned to the hight as if to wate our arrival or to defend themselves. I calculated on their number being nearly or quite equal to that of their horses, that our runing would invite pursuit as it would convince them that we were their enimies and our horses were so indifferent that we could not hope to make our escape by flight, added to this Drewyer was seperated from us and I feared that his not being apprized of the indians in the event of our attempting to escape he would most probably fall a sacrefice. under these considerations I still advanced towards them; when we had arrived ~~at the distance~~ within of a quarter of a mile of them, one of them mounted his horse and rode full speed towards us, which when I discovered I halted and alighted from my horse; he came within a hundred paces halted, looked at us and turned his horse about and returned as briskly to his party as he had advanced; while he halted near us I held out my hand and becconed to him to approach but he paid no attention to my overtures. on his return to his party, they all decended the hill and mounted their horses and advanced towards us

leaving their horses behind them, we also advanced

July 22, 1806 *This plain on which we are is very high; the rocky mountains to the S.W. Of us appear but low from their base up yet are partially covered with snow nearly to their bases. There is no timber on those mountains within our view; they are very irregular and broken in their form and seem to be composed principally of clay with but little rock or stone.*

Meriwether Lewis

The mountains that Meriwether Lewis saw from the Marias River were the heart of what later became Glacier National Park. There is a pass through Glacier, Marias Pass, but it was nearly a century after Lewis and Clark crossed the Rockies before surveyors finally found it.

Lewis awoke just after dawn to the sounds of a struggle. The soldier on guard, Joseph Field, had set his rifle down, and several of the Indians tried to exploit the mistake by quietly slipping away with all four of the Americans' rifles. When Field realized what was happening, he called to his brother, Reubin, and the two took off after the Piegan who were carrying their weapons. The Fields soon caught the man, and as Reubin was trying to wrestle the guns away he stabbed the Indian in the chest, killing him almost instantly. Meanwhile, Lewis and George Drouillard were trying to get their own rifles back. Drouillard wrestled his free from an Indian who was trying to take it, while Lewis drew his pistol and forced another Piegan to drop his rifle. Having regained their weapons, the Americans then moved to stop the Blackfeet from stealing their horses. This led to a brief exchange of gunfire in which Lewis wounded another of the Piegan, perhaps fatally, before they fled.

Lewis and his men were safe for the moment but were still in a frightening position. They were well over a hundred miles (160km)

from any of their companions. The Blackfeet, on the other hand, had said they were part of a "large band" camped near the main branch of Marias River, so more Indians could attack at any time. What really worried Lewis, though, was that the Blackfeet might attack the men he had left at the Falls, who by now should have been joined by those from Ordway's contingent bringing the canoes downstream. These men knew nothing about the skirmish that had occurred and might be caught completely off guard by vengeful Blackfeet.

Taking their pick of the remaining horses and helping themselves to the Indians' food, Lewis' squad began riding as fast as they could toward the mouth of Marias River, where they hoped to find the canoes. By Lewis' reckoning, they rode ninety miles (145km) that day, stopping twice for meals and to rest their horses and pushing on until 2 A.M. They were up again at dawn. Lewis confessed, "I was so soar from my ride yesterday that I could scarcely stand." The others were just as sore, but they saddled their horses and started to ride. Shortly before 9 A.M., as they approached the Missouri, they heard scattered gunshots, which they took to be the sound of their companions hunting, and made for "this joyfull sound." After riding 120 miles (193km) in a little over twenty-four hours, Lewis found the men he had left at the Falls plus those under Sergeant Ordway, who had gone with Clark and come downstream with the canoes. There was still no time to relax. Knowing the Blackfeet might be in hot pursuit, Lewis and his saddle-sore companions turned their horses loose, threw their saddles in the river, and clambered aboard the canoes. Then, wrote Sergeant Ordway, "we proced on with as much speed as possible."

Once it was clear he had escaped the Blackfeet, Lewis relaxed a bit but still hurried to catch his partner. He was worried he might not reach the Yellowstone in time to rendezvous with Clark and that the expedition would still be divided as they approached Teton Sioux territory. To increase his travel time each day, Lewis ordered the men to cook enough each night for that day's supper as well as the next day's breakfast and midday meal. "By this means," he calculated, "we forward our journey at least 12 or 15 miles [19 or 24km] Pr. day." Pushing downstream now at seventy to eighty miles (112.5 to 129km) a day, Lewis reached the Yellowstone on August 7, and saw when he got there that he had missed Clark, though he did not know by how much. He found a campsite he estimated had been vacant a week and fragmentary notes from his friend. "I found a paper on a pole...," wrote Lewis, "which mearly contained my name in the hand wrighting of Capt. C." He also found an undated piece of a note explaining that Clark had decided to wait farther downstream because game was scarce and mosquitoes were not. Lewis immediately set sail again in the hope of finding Clark by nightfall. Late the next day Lewis had still not caught up to Clark and called off the chase. "Not finding Capt. Clark I knew not what calculation to make with rispect to his halting and therefore determined to proceed as tho' he was not before me and leave the rest to the chapter of accedents."

Ordway's Journey

Clark had set out from Travelers' Rest the same morning Lewis did—July 3—but went south, toward the headwaters of the Missouri and the canoes that the Corps had left there when they went west. With him were eighteen soldiers, York, Charbonneau, Sacagawea, and Sacagawea and Charbonneau's young son. Five days later they reached the canoes and a cache in which they had buried a variety of supplies—including tobacco. The men had not had tobacco in months and earlier that year had been making do with substitutes made from bark. When they approached the cache, wrote Clark, "the most of the Party with me being chewers of Tobacco became So impatient to be chewing it that they Scercely gave themselves time to take their Saddles off their horses before they were off to the deposit."

The next morning, with their cravings satisfied, Clark and his men raised the Corps' canoes and readied them for use. Sergeant Ordway and nine other men were to ferry the boats downstream, picking up some of Lewis'

This print from Patrick Gass' journal shows one of the constant dangers that threatened both the lives and the success of the men in the Corps of Discovery. Many members could not swim and risked drowning on the several occasions when boats in the expedition sank. An even greater disaster, though, would have been the loss of maps, journals, and other essential papers. This is why Jefferson ordered Lewis and Clark to keep separate journals: "to guard, by multiplying them, against the accidental loses to which they will be exposed."

Pompy's Tower, near Billings, Montana, bears the only known mark of Lewis and Clark's passing. Though the two captains often carved their names or initials in trees along the route, all of those signs disappeared along with the trees bearing them. At Pompy's Tower, however, William Clark carved his name and the date in sandstone. Now protected by glass against vandals and the elements, Clark's graffiti is still visible nearly 200 years after he carved it.

men at the Falls of the Missouri and the rest at the mouth of Marias River. Ordway and Clark traveled together as far as the Three Forks—Ordway by boat and Clark with the horses. There the sergeant and his party set off on an uneventful trip down the Missouri. Arriving at the Falls on July 19, three days after Lewis set out for Marias River, Ordway's men joined forces with those left by Lewis and carried their canoes around the Falls—a job made much easier this time by the addition of horses. From the Falls, Ordway went on to rescue Lewis at the mouth of Marias River and then they continued their journey downstream, looking for Captain Clark.

Down the Yellowstone

Clark, for his part, had to find the Yellowstone first if he was going to meet Lewis and

Ordway. Led by Sacagawea, Clark and his men rode southeast from the Three Forks and struck the Yellowstone about sixty miles (96km) north of today's Yellowstone National Park. From there, he planned to canoe downstream to the Missouri, but initially he could find no trees large enough to make canoes. He briefly considered buffalo-skin boats but was afraid they would be too hard to manage on such a rapid and unfamiliar river, so he continued riding down the Yellowstone and looking for suitable trees. After several days of searching, he found two trees that were just big enough to make a pair of long narrow canoes, and when he lashed the two together they were stable enough to carry his party and its equipment.

With the canoes finally ready on July 24, Clark had no further need of his horses and directed Sergeant Pryor and three men to take the horses to Mandan country. Pryor was to leave most of the animals with the Mandan but take a dozen with him in search of Hugh Heney, the North West Company trader with connections to the Teton Sioux. If Pryor found Heney, he was to give Heney the horses as an inducement for the trader to encourage the Tetons to send a delegation to Washington. Transporting the horses promised to be a challenge. These were Indian ponies trained by their previous owners to hunt buffalo, and, according to Clark, "as Soon as they Saw the Buffalow [they] would imediately pursue them and run around them." As Clark had already seen several large herds of buffalo, he knew that Pryor would have to find some way of controlling the many riderless horses in the herd or spend all his time chasing them. Eventually, he and Pryor decided that the only solution was to send one rider well ahead of the rest to drive off any buffalo long before the horses caught sight of them.

With that problem solved, Clark and Pryor separated a few miles southwest of what is now Billings, Montana. From there, Clark and his party enjoyed a rapid and relatively uneventful journey to the Missouri. To Clark, the most noteworthy element of the trip was the sheer number of buffalo, elk, and antelope along the way. To estimate their number, he wrote the first day, "would be increditable. I shall therefore be silent on the Subject further." He could not restrain himself, though, and on later days frequently marveled at their number. One day he was even forced to land and wait an hour while a herd of buffalo crossed the river in front of him. To historians, however, the high point of Clark's voyage down the Yellowstone was his decision to carve his name again. On July 25, 1806, Clark went ashore to investigate a large rock formation he named Pompy's Tower—after Sacagawea and Charbonneau's son, Jean Baptiste, who was nicknamed Pomp by members of the expedition. The rock formation still stands, just off the interstate highway about thirty miles (48km) east of Billings, and on it Clark's name is still visible. From St. Louis to the mouth of the Columbia River, this carved name on

The Hunt for Captain Merry

As Lewis and Clark hurried down the Missouri, in September of 1806, they had no idea that less than 200 miles (320km) away was a Spanish force of some 600 militia men, regular soldiers, and Indian allies. The Spanish were on their way to the Missouri, and if the Pawnee Indians had not blocked their advance, they might well have captured the Corps of Discovery before it reached St. Louis.

Spanish officials had been trying to capture "Mr. Merry Weather Lewis, Captain of the Army of the United States" since the moment he left Camp Dubois. In March of 1804, two months before Lewis and Clark started up the Missouri, orders went out from the military governor of Louisiana "to arrest the referred to Captain Merry and his followers...and to seize their papers and instruments." Over the next two years, four different expeditions left Santa Fe in search of the Americans. The first, in August 1804, got as far as the Platte River, in central Nebraska, but by then Lewis and Clark were already well north of the Platte. A second Spanish effort, in October 1805, quickly ended when Indians attacked it, while a third, in April 1806, apparently failed because of mass desertions.

The final Spanish effort came in the summer of 1806, when Lieutenant Facundo Melgares left Santa Fe with 105 Spanish soldiers, 400 New Mexico milita men, and 100 Indians. Melgares and half of his men reached a Pawnee village on the Republican River, in south-central Nebraska, around September 1. Had they continued another week, the Spanish might well have reached the junction of the Missouri and Platte Rivers just as Lewis and Clark arrived, on September 9. Melgares did not push on, though. His column had already lost many of its horses to Indian raiders, the Pawnee objected to his presence, and his men were anxious to go home. Melgares returned to Santa Fe, Lewis and Clark reached St. Louis, and what might have been a very different ending to the story of America's most famous explorers never came to pass.

Pompy's Tower is the only surviving physical evidence of Lewis and Clark's passing.

On August 3 Clark reached the Missouri. Finding no sign of Lewis, who was still well upstream, he settled down to wait. The next day, however, he decided to move as there were no buffalo at the mouth of the Yellowstone and the mosquitoes were ruthless. Leaving Lewis a note—fragments of which Lewis found three days later—he continued slowly down the Missouri, stopping at times to wait for his partner to catch up. Five days after reaching the Missouri, on August 8, Clark thought the wait was over when two boats came into view. To his surprise, though, the newcomers were not Lewis and his men; they were Sergeant Pryor and the horse wranglers Clark had sent to the Mandan. Two nights after

Pryor and Clark had separated, the entire herd of horses were stolen. Pryor, realizing he had no hope of recapturing the horses on foot, led his men north to the Yellowstone River. There the men killed a buffalo and used its hide to make two Mandan-style bullboats, in which skin is stretched over hemispheric frames built of sticks. In these they floated down the Yellowstone "without taking a drop of water" and then down the Missouri until they caught up with Clark.

Reunion

Four days later, on August 12, Lewis finally caught up. His arrival was hardly what anyone expected, though. He was stretched out on his

stomach recovering from a bullet wound. The day before, Lewis had gone out hunting with Corps member Pierre Cruzatte. According to Clark, Cruzatte was an excellent man in whom both captains had great faith, but he was also "near Sighted and has the use of but one eye." Moving through a thicket, Cruzatte saw and fired at what he thought was an elk but was actually Lewis dressed in clothes made of elk skin. The ball struck Lewis in the left leg, passed through his thigh, and cut across his right buttock. Once everyone realized that Indians were not attacking the party and calm was restored, Lewis was relieved to find that the bullet had struck neither bone nor artery, and he assured Clark when they met that "his wound was slight." It was, however, quite painful and kept Lewis from walking for two

weeks. It was nearly a month before Clark declared Lewis "entirely recovered."

The reunion was a relief to both captains. After close calls in the weeks apart, the Corps of Discovery was now safely reassembled, and everyone could relax more than they had at any time since leaving Travelers' Rest. It was also obvious now that they were entering the home stretch; the day of their reunion the captains met a pair of American fur traders on the Missouri—the first white men outside the Corps they had seen in more than a year. In fact, though no one knew it yet, members of the true Lewis and Clark Expedition—those who went to the coast—had just three more days together. On August 14, 1806, Lewis and Clark arrived back at the Mandan villages, and the next day the Corps began to disband.

Chapter Eleven

Home Again

ETURNING TO MANDAN COUNTRY MEANT THE Corps of Discovery was almost home, and members of the expedition were already thinking about life after the adventure of a lifetime. The first member of the Corps to leave was John Colter. Joseph Dickson and Forrest Hancock, the traders whom Lewis and Clark had met just a few days earlier, offered Colter a share in their fur trading venture. Colter knew as much as any white man alive about the Upper Missouri and Yellowstone River Valleys, and his knowledge would be invaluable to Dickson and Hancock. They made Colter what Clark called "a very advantagious" offer, and Colter asked the captains to release him from his enlistment. The captains were willing to let Colter go only if every other soldier in the Corps agreed not to request a similar release

NEBRASKA

Platte River

KANSAS

IOWA

Sgt. Floyd's grave

MISSOURI

Mississippi River

Missouri River

St. Louis

Capacity of...interpretes," and he wrote several days later that she "diserved a greater reward for her attention and services...than we had it in our power to give her at the Mandans." Still, she never received any compensation.

Lewis and Clark spent three days with the Mandan, trying to convince the Indians to send a delegation to Washington. Finally, one of the chiefs, Sheheke, agreed to go with them to meet "our Great Father," but only if he could bring with him one of his wives, his son, an interpreter he trusted, and the interpreter's wife and children. The captains reluctantly agreed to the demand, and after a quick visit to the remains of Fort Mandan, which had burned since their departure, they resumed their voyage down the Missouri.

Down the River to St. Louis

Once they left the Mandan, every member of the expedition seems to have realized that their great adventure was drawing to a close. They were still more than fifteen hundred miles (2,400km) from St. Louis, but the frontier had moved upstream while they were gone. Almost every week they met boats carrying white men upstream to trade with the Indians. Long before Lewis and Clark returned, Jefferson's dream of American traders heading up the Missouri came true. And long before they reached St. Louis, members of the Corps found the trappings of civilization. From the traders they met they obtained food, clothing to replace their rotting leather garments, tobacco, and whiskey—the men's first liquor in more than a year. They also obtained news of the world since their departure, including news about themselves: that they had been killed or captured by the Spanish!

Sensing that the end was near, everyone tried to make the most of the time they had left. The captains made a final effort to capture animal specimens for the president, stopping for a full day so that the hunters could look for

PAGE 136: *By the time Lewis and Clark returned to the Plains, summer was in full swing. Members of the expedition had little time for flowers, though. They were so anxious to get home by then that they asked the captains not to stop—even to hunt.*
ABOVE: *Sailing with the Missouri's current, the expedition raced downstream to St. Louis, arriving there on September 23, 1806, 28 months and 7000 miles (11,200km) after their departure.*

before they reached St. Louis. The others agreed, wishing Colter "every Suckcess," and a few days later he set out with Dickson and Hancock, "determined to Stay untill they make a fortune." Colter had been a valuable member of the expedition, and in recognition of his service Lewis and Clark not only consented to his release, but equipped him with powder, lead, and other items and kept him on the Corps' payroll until they officially disbanded later that year.

The same day Colter left, the captains settled with Charbonneau, paying him $500 "for his Services as an enterpreter" and for the horse and tepee he had provided the Corps. In addition, Clark offered Charbonneau and his family passage downstream and help settling in Illinois country, an offer that Charbonneau declined as he had no family in Illinois and no way of making a living there. Clark even offered to take and raise Charbonneau and Sacagawea's son, Jean Baptiste, "in Such a manner as I thought proper," but agreed that would have to wait until the child was weaned. There was no mention that day of paying Sacagawea for her work. Clark did specifically acknowledge that she had accompanied the Corps "in the antelope, mule deer, and prairie dogs. The men, Ordway wrote, tried to kill extra buffalo and saved all the buffalo horns they could find "to take to the States as they would make excelent k[n]ife and fork handles." The Corps also stopped to visit the grave of Sergeant Floyd, the only member who would never go home again. Finding that the grave had been opened, they refilled it, paid their respects, and continued on their way.

By mid-September the boats were traveling "with great velocity." They had the Missouri's current in their favor and the men were pulling on their oars, but neither of these was the main reason for their speed. The men were now so anxious to get home that they asked the captains not to stop to hunt. For those last few days they were willing to live on papaws, a fruit common in the region, which could quickly be gathered along the shore, if it got them home just a few hours sooner.

On September 20, 1806, they saw cows for the first time since their journey began—"a joyfull Sight," reported Clark. Late that afternoon they arrived in La Charette, a "little french Village" and the westernmost white settlement on the Missouri. The Corps and the trading boats that were docked at La Charette exchanged salutes, and the men went ashore to visit. According to Clark, "every person, both

As the Corps of Discovery hurried down the Missouri toward St. Louis, it passed out of the distinctive Great Plains environment and back into the more familiar Eastern woodlands.

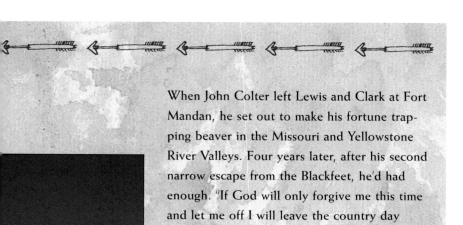

When John Colter left Lewis and Clark at Fort Mandan, he set out to make his fortune trapping beaver in the Missouri and Yellowstone River Valleys. Four years later, after his second narrow escape from the Blackfeet, he'd had enough. "If God will only forgive me this time and let me off I will leave the country day after tomorrow—and be damned if I ever come into again."

Back in St. Louis, he sat down again with William Clark to fill in some of the blanks on a map of the West that Clark was preparing for publication. Colter had spent the winter of 1807–1808 on a spectacular tour of the American wilderness. From a trading post in southern Montana, he had circled through northwestern Wyoming, southern Idaho, and southwestern Montana. On the way, he told Clark, he crossed streams of water so hot they never froze, found pools of boiling mud that reeked of sulfur, and saw great jets of water exploding out of the earth.

Clark knew Colter and probably believed what he told him. Others who heard him did not. Long after Colter died, in 1813, people retold his tall tales and laughed at his stories of geysers and boiling mud; "Colter's Hell" they called it. Not until after the Civil War did surveyors and photographers rediscover what Colter had seen during that incredible winter of 1807. Colter's Hell, it turned out, was very real; northwestern Wyoming contained a number of very active geothermal regions. In 1872, Congress made one of them the United States' first national park: Yellowstone National Park. Whether or not John Colter actually entered what is now Yellowstone National Park will probably never be known, but his name is forever linked with it.

French and americans Seem to express great pleasure at our return, and acknowledge them selves much astonished in Seeing us return." It was much the same when they reached St. Charles the next day. They were warmly welcomed by the townsfolk, who were "excessively polite" but "could hardly belive that it was us for they had heard and had believed that we were all dead and were forgotten."

And then, twenty-eight months after it started, their great journey was over. On Thursday, September 23, the Corps of Discovery reached St. Louis again. "They really have the appearance of Robinson Crusoes," wrote one witness, "dressed entirely in buckskins." The fullest account of their joyful return, though, comes from the journal of Sergeant Ordway:

> About 12 oclock we arived in Site of St Louis fired three Rounds as we approached the Town and landed oppocit the center of the Town, the people gathred on the Shore and Hizzared three cheers. we unloaded the canoes and carried the baggage all up to a store house in Town drew out the canoes then the party all considerable much rejoiced that we have the Expedition Completed and now we look for boarding in Town and wait for our Settlement and then we entend to return to our native homes to See our parents once more as we have been so long from them.— finis.

John Colter tried to describe the wonderous things he had seen—such as this geyser in Yellowstone National Park. Many, though, refused to believe such things existed and mockingly dubbed the Yellowstone region "Colter's Hell."

September 20, 1806 *The party being extreemly anxious to get down ply their ores very well, we Saw Some cows on the bank which was a joyfull Sight to the party and Caused a Shout to be raised for joy at PM we came in Sight of the little french Villiage called Charriton the men raised a Shout and Sprung upon their ores and we soon landed opposit to the Villiage.*

William Clark

As the Corps of Discovery descended the Missouri its mighty current hurried them back toward St. Louis. They had often made just ten miles (16km) a day going upstream; going down they sometimes covered seventy miles (112km) in a single day.

Chapter Twelve

Passing into Legend

WITHIN HOURS OF THEIR RETURN, Lewis and Clark had begun to fashion their place in history. The mail from St. Louis had already gone by then, and with it at least one account of the Corps' return that was later published in several newspapers, but the captains wanted the world to hear directly from them as soon as possible. They rushed a note to the postmaster in nearby Cahokia, who had not yet sent his scheduled post to the East, asking him to hold the mail there until noon the next day. Early the next morning they wrote at least two letters of their own. The captains knew these letters would be published throughout the nation and wanted them to reflect well on themselves, their men, and what they had done. In such an important situation, Clark had little confidence in himself as a

was a summary of Lewis' letter to the president. From Washington, the article traveled south, north, and east; it was reprinted in Norfolk on November 3, in Boston on November 6, and in London on December 3. Close behind it came a longer report—Clark's letter to his brother—that had actually been in print first but had not reached Washington by the time Jefferson's news was released. Clark's letter was first run in the Frankfort, Kentucky, *Palladium* on October 9 and as far as historians can tell was the first printed account anywhere of the Lewis and Clark Expedition. From Frankfort it moved east and appeared in Washington and other eastern cities about a week after the presidential announcement published by the *National Intelligencer.*

Tributes to Lewis and Clark

Throughout the United States, the public response to Lewis and Clark's return was generally positive. In spite of the bitter political divisions in the country and Lewis and Clark's connection to the president, most American newspapers treated the expedition as a national triumph. Even in New England, home to many of Jefferson's most bitter enemies, papers reprinted the *Palladium's* statement that, whatever differences of opinion might exist about the benefits of the expedition, "we are persuaded all think and feel alike, on the courage, perseverance, and prudent deportment displayed by this adventurous party. They are entitled to, and will receive the plaudits of their countrymen."

Foreign reaction was not always so favorable. When the *National Intelligencer's* story was reprinted in London, it prompted an immediate charge of fraud. A reader of the *London Times* wrote that the story "purporting to be an Extract of a Letter from Captain LEWIS" had to be a hoax. The reader himself had recently received a letter from "a Gentleman of unquestionable veracity" in Canada, who reported that Lewis and Clark had spent the winter of

writer, so Lewis, who was more educated and wrote in the genteel style of the day, wrote for both men. Over his own name he sent a report to the president, while on Clark's behalf he drafted a letter that Clark copied and sent to his brother.

The Early News

These two letters contained the first detailed accounts of the Lewis and Clark Expedition. They spread news of the Corps' success as rapidly as technology would permit. It was fitting that much of the world first heard the news through Thomas Jefferson, the expedition's prime mover. The *National Intelligencer,* a Washington newspaper that often served as the unofficial voice of the Jefferson administration, wrote on October 27, "It is with the sincerest pleasure, that we announce to our fellow citizens, the arrival of CAPTAIN LEWIS, with his exploring party, at St. Lewis." What followed

LEFT: *Twenty-six years after his return to St. Louis, William Clark posed for this portrait by George Catlin. Clark was sixty-two at the time, was still active in Indian affairs, and was already one of the Lewis and Clark Expedition's last survivors. So many of its members died so young that some people considered the Corps of Discovery cursed.*

OPPOSITE: ***One of the few surviving artifacts of the Lewis and Clark expedition is this buffalo robe on which a Mandan artist painted his account of a battle between a Mandan/Hidatsa force and one made up of Arikaras and Teton Sioux. Lewis and Clark sent the robe from Fort Mandan to President Jefferson, and Jefferson may have displayed it at Monticello before it finally ended up at Harvard.***

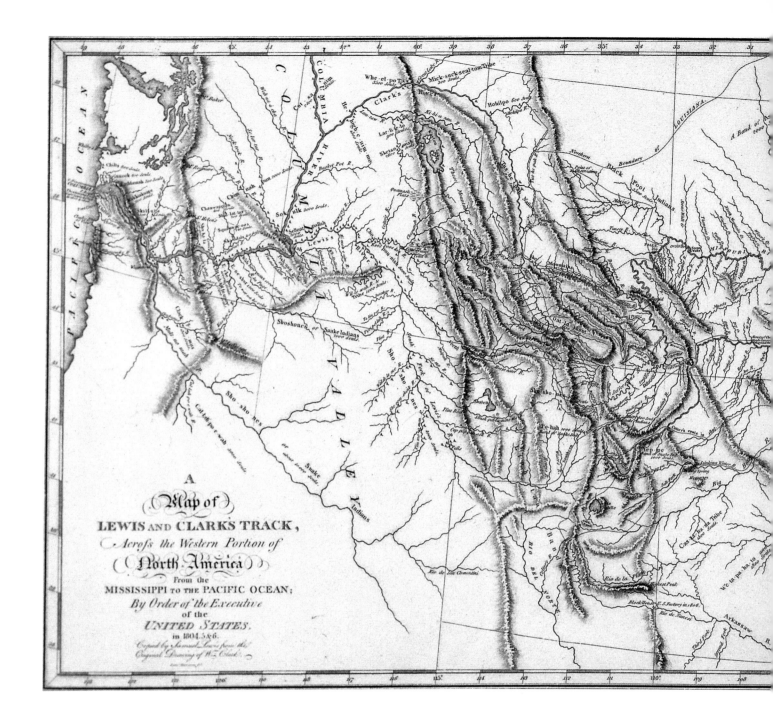

1805–1806 near the source of the Missouri
River, not at Fort Clatsop. Thus, the *Times* reader implied, they could not possibly have gone
from there to the coast and back to St. Louis
by September, and he pointed this out "in order
that an opportunity may be afforded of establishing the truth of a fact so interesting to
geography, and indeed to the public at large."

Back in America, however, Lewis and
Clark were hailed as heroes. Two nights after
their arrival in St. Louis, they were honored at
a dinner and ball. In the style of the day, guests
drank toast after toast—to the President,
Congress, Lewis and Clark, their men, the

Missouri River, and even "the fair daughters of
Louisiana." The same pattern was followed in
other towns once the captains left St. Louis for
Washington, D.C. Clark did not make it to
Washington in time for the banquet held there
as he was delayed in Virginia courting the
young woman who soon became his wife. Lewis
was in Washington, however, as the guests were
treated to nine stanzas of "On the Discoveries
of Captain Lewis"—a poem written by Joel
Barlow. Barlow also proposed to Jefferson that
the Columbia River be renamed the Lewis, and
later that year Charles Willson Peale placed a
wax figure of Lewis in his Philadelphia museum.

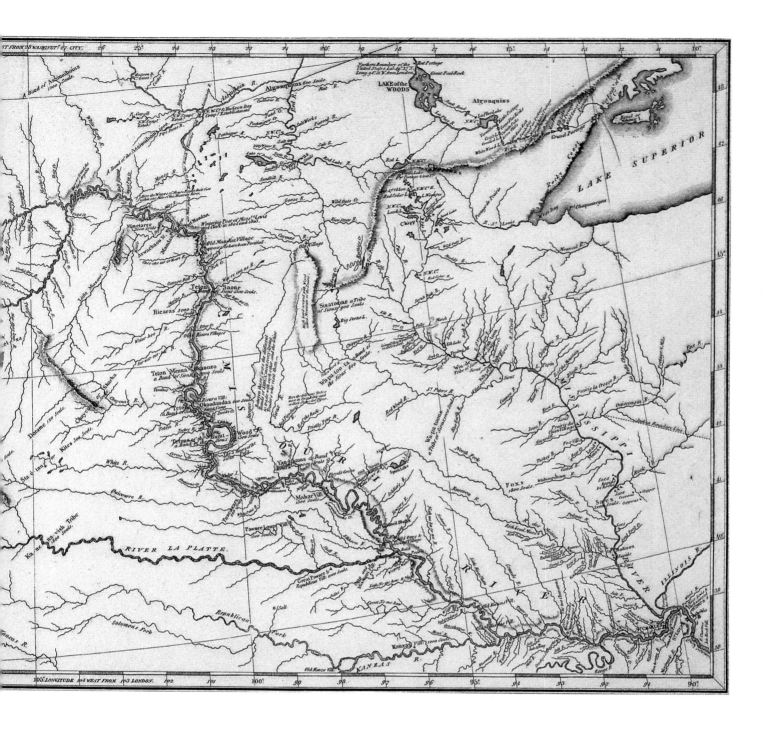

This flood of tributes to Lewis and Clark was finally too much for at least one of their contemporaries to bear. John Quincy Adams, then a U.S. senator from Massachusetts, was an ardent nationalist and in later years played an active role in America's westward expansion. In 1807, however, he was sick of Lewis and Clark. The final straw seems to have been Barlow's poetic tribute to Meriwether Lewis. It prompted a response from Adams that was published anonymously in March 1807:

Good people listen to my tale,
'Tis nothing but what true is;

I'll tell you of the mighty deeds
Achieved by Captain Lewis—
How starting from the Atlantick shore
By fair and easy motion,
He journied, <u>*all the way by land,*</u>
Until he met the ocean

Books on the Expedition

Adams was in the minority. Public interest in Lewis and Clark was still high, judging by the books that were quickly published to capitalize

One of the great legacies of the Lewis and Clark Expedition was the knowledge it provided of western geography. This map produced by William Clark filled in many of the spaces that had been empty or conjectural when the Corps of Discovery set out.

on it. Patrick Gass, a sergeant in the Corps of Discovery, was the first to publish. In 1807 he released an account of the expedition based on the journal he kept. It sold well and for several years was the only book available. Robert Frazer, a private in the Corps, also planned a book in 1807 but it never came out. Nor did the work most eagerly awaited: Meriwether Lewis' projected three-volume account of the Lewis and Clark Expedition. Lewis announced in the spring of 1807 that he intended to publish a map of the west and the expedition's route to the Pacific later that year, the first volume of text in January 1808, and the remaining volumes as quickly as possible. When Lewis' work did not come out on time, and then never came out, other printers met the demand for information with reprints of Gass' book and odd hybrids made up of bits of Gass' work, some of Clark's letters, and items written by various people with no connection to the expedition at all.

Not until 1814 did an "official" history of the Lewis and Clark Expedition appear in print. Its author, Nicholas Biddle, had full access to the journals of both captains and after reading them spent days interviewing Clark to fill in gaps and reconcile inconsistencies in the diaries. Biddle continued to correspond with Clark while writing his book and was further assisted by George Shannon, a member of the expedition. When it came out, Biddle's work was the definitive account of the Lewis and Clark Expedition and remained so until the end of the nineteenth century. By the time it came out, though, interest was waning in Lewis and Clark. The War of 1812 was at its peak then, and America was finding new heroes to admire.

What Happened to the Corps

The Corps of Discovery officially disbanded in October 1806, less than three weeks after its return to St. Louis. Its boats and equipment were sold at auction and the men were discharged. Each member of the Corps received a grant of land for his service and back pay since his date of enlistment; for the privates this came to $166.67 and for the sergeants about $250, thirty-three months worth of earnings. Then they scattered to every corner of the North American continent.

About a third simply disappeared from the historical record, and we have no idea where they went or what they did. Another third settled in what were then the western states—Indiana, Illinois, and Missouri—and lived quiet lives. Most became farmers, though one at least, George Shannon, became a lawyer and a state politician. The final third followed the example of John Colter and went west again as trappers and traders after mustering out of the Corps. Of these men, Colter is certainly the best known. After leaving the expedition shortly before it returned to St. Louis, he spent four more years in the Upper Missouri and Yellowstone River Valleys. He may have been the first white man to visit what is now Yellowstone National Park, and he spent at least one winter on the Idaho side of the Grand

This title page is from an edition of Nicholas Biddle's history of the Lewis and Clark Expedition. Though Biddle was not a member of the party, he had unparalleled access to the Corps' writings and its members. Lewis and Clark's journals remained in his possession for years, William Clark granted him a series of lengthy interviews, and George Shannon, who had been a member of the expedition, helped Biddle compile his work.

HISTORY

OF

THE EXPEDITION

UNDER THE COMMAND OF

CAPTAINS LEWIS AND CLARK,

TO

THE SOURCES OF THE MISSOURI,

THENCE

ACROSS THE ROCKY MOUNTAINS

AND DOWN THE

RIVER COLUMBIA TO THE PACIFIC OCEAN.

PERFORMED DURING THE YEARS 1804—5—6.

By order of the

GOVERNMENT OF THE UNITED STATES.

PREPARED FOR THE PRESS

BY PAUL ALLEN, ESQUIRE.

IN TWO VOLUMES.

VOL. I.

PHILADELPHIA:

PUBLISHED BY BRADFORD AND INSKEEP; AND ABM. H. INSKEEP, NEWYORK.

J. Maxwell, Printer.

1814.

December 2, 1806 *The expedition of Messr. Lewis & Clarke, for exploring the river Missouri, and the best communication from that to the Pacific ocean, has had all the success which could have been expected. they have traced the Missouri nearly to it's source, descended the Columbia to the Pacific ocean, ascertained with accuracy the geography of that interesting communication across our continent, learnt the character of the country, of it's commerce & inhabitants, and it is but justice to say that Messrs. Lewis and Clarke and their brave companions, have, by this arduos service, deserved well of their country.*

Thomas Jefferson

This portrait of Meriwether Lewis, by Charles B. J. F. de Saint-Mémin, was painted in 1807, after the explorer's return. It shows Lewis as he may have looked at one of the Lewis and Clark Expedition's critical moments. He posed for the work in a fur tippet that was probably given to him by Cameahwait, Sacagawea's brother and the Shoshone chief whose help was critical to the expedition's successful crossing of the Rocky Mountains.

Tetons. He was also captured by Blackfeet Indians near the Three Forks but escaped when they chose to give him a running start before killing him. After all his hair-raising adventures, Colter returned to Missouri in 1810 and settled down to farm. Several of those who followed him were less fortunate: John Potts was captured by the Blackfeet with Colter but did not escape; George Drouillard was also killed by the Blackfeet; and John Collins was killed by the Arikaras.

Wherever they went, members of the Corps did not live very long. One of the first to go was Meriwether Lewis. The young hero had been appointed governor of Upper Louisiana soon after his return to Washington, but his tenure was a disaster. He did not even return to St. Louis, the territory's capital, until a year after he was appointed, and then he devoted little time or energy to the post. Nor did he

work on his planned history of the Lewis and Clark Expedition. He was far too busy speculating in land, entering the fur trade, and trying to sort out the increasingly tangled details of his public and private finances. He was also sliding into depression and alcoholism. In September 1809 he left St. Louis for Washington but never got there. During the night of October 11, at an inn southwest of Nashville, Tennessee, he committed suicide. He was thirty-five years old.

Lewis' friend and co-commander, William Clark, had a long and satisfying career after his return from the Pacific. He filled a number of government positions in what became Missouri Territory and then the state of Missouri, but he was best known as the superintendent of Indian affairs in the trans-Mississippi region. In that capacity he continued to deal with many of the individuals and tribes he first met on his famous expedition and retained their friendship and respect. He married twice and fathered five children. About 1825 Clark tried to learn the fate of his companions and found that most were already dead. At the time Clark himself died, in St. Louis in 1838, only three other members of the official Corps of Discovery are known to have been alive.

Those who traveled with Lewis and Clark but were not considered members of the Corps did a little bit better. Toussaint Charbonneau worked briefly as an Indian trader and then spent years as a government interpreter during Clark's tenure as superintendent of Indian affairs. He was dead by 1843. His wife, Sacagawea, probably died in 1812. Their son, Jean Baptiste, did go to live with William Clark and was educated in St. Louis. Through Clark he met a traveling German prince and went with him back to Germany for several years before returning to St. Louis in 1829. He then became a guide and interpreter in the Missouri Valley for many years before migrating to California in search of gold. He died in Oregon in 1866. York stayed with William Clark for at least a few years after their return. He was freed from slavery in 1811 and went

Millions of Americans still follow the trail blazed by Lewis and Clark, passing the same Great Plains and Rocky Mountains the Corps of Discovery saw. In the nineteenth century, trappers, miners, and farmers followed their trail to develop the West. Now tourists admire the scenery and wildlife first described by Lewis and Clark.

into business hauling freight. The business failed, though, and York was dead by 1832.

One by one, the last survivors died—Alexander Willard in 1865, Jean Baptiste Charbonneau in 1866, and Patrick Gass in 1870. Gass was the last to die, and with his death the nation lost its final living link to the Lewis and Clark Expedition. All that remained were the artifacts, specimens, and journals they brought back, most of which lay forgotten in various museums by 1870.

Now, almost two centuries after Lewis and Clark set off to cross the continent, many of the artifacts and specimens have also been lost or destroyed. What remains are the journals. They consist of two dozen small volumes deposited after Lewis' death with the American Philosophical Society in Philadelphia. Historians rediscovered them there in the 1890s; they were finally published for the first time in 1901—just in time for the centennial of the expedition; and now, as we approach the expedition's bicentennial, a new, even better edition, is being published. Through these journals Lewis and Clark will live forever.

Kept today at the American Philosophical Society, Lewis and Clark's journals, and those of the other Corps members, are among the United States' most treasured documents.

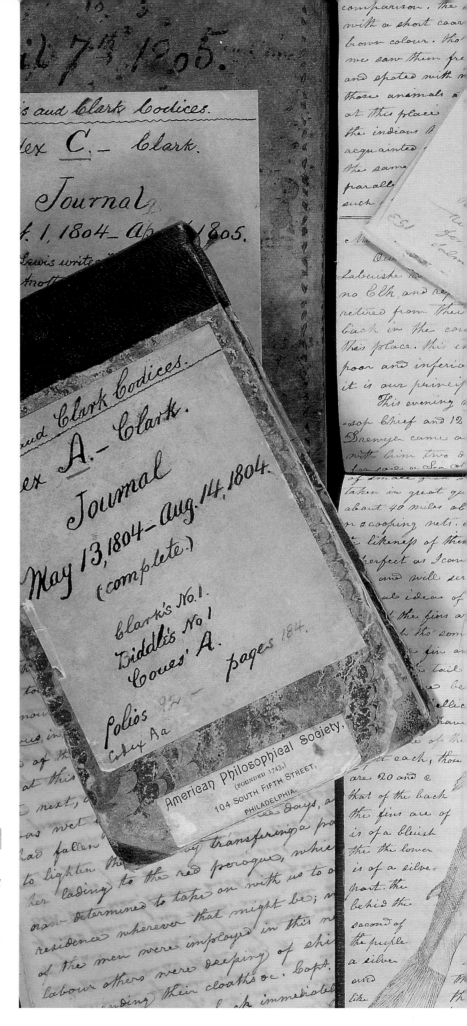

Further Reading

John Logan Allen, *Passage Through the Garden: Lewis and Clark and the Image of the American Northwest* (University of Illinois Press, 1975).

Stephen E. Ambrose, *Undaunted Courage: Meriwether Lewis. Thomas Jefferson, and the Opening of the American West* (Simon & Schuster, 1996).

Robert B. Betts, *In Search of York: The Slave Who Went to the Pacific with Lewis and Clark* (Colorado Associated University Press, 1985).

Eldon G. Chuinard, *Only One Man Died: The Medical Aspects of the Lewis and Clark Expedition* (Arthur H. Clark, 1970).

Paul Russell Cutright, *A History of the Lewis and Clark Journals* (University of Oklahoma Press, 1976).

Paul Russell Cutright, *Lewis and Clark: Pioneering Naturalists* (University of Illinois Press, 1969).

Albert Furtwangler, *Acts of Discovery: Visions of America in the Lewis and Clark Journals* (University of Illinois Press, 1993).

Barry M. Gough, *First Across the Continent: Sir Alexander Mackensie* (University of Oklahoma Press, 1997).

David Freeman Hawke, *Those Tremendous Mountains: The Story of the Lewis and Clark Expedition* (W.W. Norton & Co., 1980).

Harold P. Howard, *Sacajawea* (University of Oklahoma Press, 1971).

Donald Jackson (ed.), *Letters of the Lewis and Clark Expedition with Related Documents, 1783–1854* (University of Illinois Press, 1978).

Gary E. Moulton (ed.), *Atlas of the Lewis and Clark Expedition* (University of Nebraska Press, 1983).

Gary E. Moulton (ed.), *The Journals of the Lewis and Clark Expedition* (University of Nebraska Press, 1986–).

James P. Ronda, *Lewis and Clark Among the Indians* (University of Nebraska Press, 1984).

Gerald S. Snyder, *In the Footsteps of Lewis and Clark* (National Geographic Society, 1970).

Jerome O. Steffen, *William Clark: Jeffersonian Man on the Frontier* (University of Oklahoma Press, 1977).

Photo Credits

Courtesy of the American Philosophical Society, Philadelphia, PA: endpapers, pp. 58, 61, 79, 116, 127, 148-149, 154-155

Art Resource, NY/©Giraudon: p. 13; ©Erich Lessing: p. 47; ©National Museum of American Art, Washington, D.C.: pp. 39, 46, 49, 53 top, 54, 55, 56, 91; ©National Portrait Gallery, Smithsonian Institution: p. 147

©Ed Cooper Photography: pp. 2, 10, 62, 76, 83, 88, 92, 93, 100, 104, 107 top, 110-111, 112, 115, 122, 136

©John Elk III: pp. 7, 50, 60, 73, 82, 107 bottom, 132, 139, 144

©Bill Farnsworth: pp. 29, 66, 71, 85, 134-135

Courtesy of the Independence National Historical Park Collection, Philadelphia, PA: pp. 25, 30

©1985 Mort Kunstler, Inc.: pp. 96-97, 120-121

Courtesy of the Library of Congress: p. 131

Courtesy of the Missouri Historical Society Archives: pp. 43, 68, 70, 72, 94, 95, 103, 105, 108 all, 109

Courtesy of the Montana Historical Society: p. 57 (gift of the artist); ©Mackay Collection: pp. 74-75, ©John Reddy: pp. 80-81

North Wind Photo Archives: pp. 14, 15, 31, 34, 69, 119, 150

Courtesy of the Peabody Museum, Harvard University; Photo by Hillel Burger: p. 146

©National Museum of American History, Smithsonian Institution: p. 130 (photo # 95-3550)

Stock Montage, Inc.: p. 151; ©The Newberry Library: pp. 48, 65, 125, 126

©Tom Till: pp. 17, 18-19, 20-21, 22, 32-33, 36, 44-45, 53 bottom, 118, 128-129, 140-141

©Jeffrey L. Torretta: p. 98

The Wildlife Collection/©Tim Crosby: p. 106; ©Michael H. Francis: pp. 86-87; ©Henry H. Holdsworth: pp. 152-153; ©Tom Till: pp. 35, 142-143

Courtesy of the Yale Collection of Western Americana, Beinecke Rare Book and Manuscript Library: pp. 27, 40, 41, 42

©Oliver Yourke: pp. 8-9, 38, 52, 64, 78, 90, 102, 114, 124, 138

his insolence I would tom

withdrew apparently mue

my repast on dog) without

dinner we continued our

of Colter's Creek about

where we sunk the 1st.

river last fall. we enca

this creek at a little dista

Chopunnish nation hav

one of these lodges contai

was much the largest

feet long and about 15 wi

in the form of the roof

ber of small doors on ea